A Different
Kind of crazy

A DIFFERENT KIND OF CRAZY

Living the Way Jesus Lived

LAWRENCE W. WILSON

wesleyan
publishing
house

Indianapolis, Indiana

Copyright © 2007 by Lawrence W. Wilson
Published by Wesleyan Publishing House
Indianapolis, Indiana
Printed in the United States of America
ISBN: 978-0-89827-348-9

Library of Congress Cataloging-in-Publication Data

Wilson, Lawrence W., 1959-
  A different kind of crazy : living the way Jesus lived / Lawrence W.
Wilson.
      p. cm.
  ISBN 978-0-89827-348-9
  1. Christian life. 2. Jesus Christ--Example. I. Title.
  BV4501.3.W555 2007
  248.4--dc22
                                        2007014313

For Uriah and Lydia,

In the hope that they will carry the light of

Christ into the next generation

I have one deep, supreme desire,
that I may be like Jesus.

—Thomas Chisholm

contents

	Preface	9
	Acknowledgments	13
1.	Authenticity	15
2.	Vision	23
3.	Significance	35
4.	Holiness	49
5.	Purity	63
6.	Forbearance	77
7.	Charity	89
8.	Spirituality	103
9.	Trust	119
10.	Tolerance	129
11.	Faith	143
12.	Kindness	155
13.	Integrity	169
14.	Commitment	183
	Afterword	195
	The Sermon on the Mount	199
	Discussion Guide	211
	Note to Readers	223

preface

I know how audacious it seems to write a book that defines the Christian life. Over the years, I've observed many people who claimed to be doing that. Most of them seemed to be describing some version of themselves. It is a powerful temptation, the urge to remake the world in one's own image. So I say at the outset that this is not a book about my own experience as a Christian, as if I were the prime example of the species.

I haven't the self-confidence of Paul, who said, "Follow me as I follow Christ." I know my sin too well. My approach here is more like that of the Baptist, who, grieved by the spiritual failure of his generation, simply pointed to Jesus, saying, "Behold, the Lamb of God."

Neither do I have the intellectual confidence of my old mentor, C. S. Lewis, who said in his preface to *Mere Christianity* that our faith must be defined in terms of its creeds, that a Christian is someone who adheres to an intellectual code, who believes what Christians believe. Jesus did not say, "Repeat after me," as if the faith were a set of arithmetic tables to be swallowed and regurgitated on command. He said, "Follow me." Jesus showed us a way of living, a way of being. He showed us the Father so that we could be like him—holy, as he is holy.

Here, then, is my thesis: To be a Christian is to live as Jesus lived, and, unlikely as it seems, ordinary people can do exactly that.

Nobody comes to a discussion of religion empty handed. We bring with us the baggage we've collected over the years. So it may help the reader to know that I am an ordained minister in The Wesleyan Church, and that I greatly value my association with this congregation of saints. It is the particular manifestation of Christ's church that gave me birth and formed my thinking about the faith. It is certain that this heritage has shaped the way I think about following Jesus. Yet while my denomination is nearly always referred to as evangelical, the older I grow the less I am inclined to accept vague and often divisive labels such as fundamentalist or emergent, mainline or evangelical to describe my own faith. Let it be like Christ—*Christian*. That should be a defining term, and a uniting one.

This book is riddled with stories from my life, all of them true. While I have changed the names and taken some liberties with the settings, each event matches my recollection. Whether I have remembered factually or only truthfully, others can decide. Also, I have related some bits of my own journey with Christ in this book, and in each case have relived the moments as they occurred. Where I have felt anger or fear or frustration at matching my life to Christ's, I've said so in the present tense. Those who wish to know whether those thoughts and emotions describe my present experience might ask my wife or my children; I've already said that I am not the prime example of Christlikeness. Yet I have grown through and beyond many of the experiences presented in this book.

Any reader who is familiar with Christ's Sermon on the Mount will recognize that it forms an outline for this writing. No other words of Christ's reveal him more clearly, and no other of his teachings are more universally recognized and admired—even by those of other religions. This is Christianity in its purest form. This book asks what those words might mean for a believer living two thousand years after Jesus spoke them. The publisher has included them as an appendix to this writing, but that order is quite wrong. These thoughts are at best an appendix to Christ's teaching. Turn now to the end of this book, and read the Sermon on the Mount. Reread it. Internalize it. Memorize it, if you can. That is authentic Christianity.

These thoughts are offered in the hope that they will cause some who do not know Jesus to put their faith in him, and those who do to think and act more like him whose name we bear.

This is my aim in writing; this is my aim in living. I invite you to join me.

acknowledgments

I t is my privilege to work each day with an outstanding team at Wesleyan Publishing House, headed by Don Cady. To Don, I say thanks for your willingness to invest in this message.

Thanks to the editorial and design team, especially Mark Moore, who edited the manuscript, Jennette ElNaggar, an able assistant and proofreader, Lyn Rayn, who designed the text, and Jim Weinmann, who got the book on the shelf.

Thanks also to Mary McNeil for editorial assistance and for lying almost as blatantly as my mother about the quality of my work; to Rich Eckley, for thinking most of these thoughts ahead of me; to Larry and Cindy Marshall, for providing insight through their example; and to Wayne and Jo Anne Lyon for being amazing people.

I am especially grateful to my parents, Norman and Nancy Wilson, whose lives have provided an example of the lessons in this book—and some of the stories. Thanks for graciously accepting your portrayal here.

Finally, to Heather, thank you for your patience as I devoted much time and attention to this project, for listening intently as I read passages to you, and for the discerning critiques that have strengthened the book. Thanks most of all for being my wife.

1

AUTHENTICITY

"His disciples came to him, and he
began to teach them. . . ."

Some . . . confuse authenticity, which they ought always to aim at, with originality, which they should never bother about.

—W. H. AUDEN

I like Jim and Barbara, but sometimes it's hard to remember why. They're in town once or twice a year on business and bring an enjoyable dollop of Hollywood glitz with them. Yet the talk of fashion and celebrities grows wearisome after a day or two, and I'm seldom sorry for their return to the Coast. We dined at El Ranchero, a kitschy Mexican restaurant on the north side of Indianapolis.

"In L.A.," Barbara began predictably, "we get the most authentic Mexican food."

"Out of this world," Jim agreed.

"I mean, it's to *die* for," Barbara whispered, as if there were some dirty secret about chimichangas.

I unfolded a napkin and put it on my lap.

"Enrique," Barbara continued, "our chef at Las Palmas, makes the most *un*believable carne asada. And the chicken mole verde? Di*vine*."

"Out of this world," Jim said again.

"Here in the Midwest," Babs waxed on, "you simply can't get good Mexican food. I mean really authentic Mexican."

"You absolutely can't get it," Jim swore, as if affirming under oath that he'd seen George W. Bush stuffing a ballot box in Cleveland.

"But this place is so *fun*," Barbara chirped with exaggerated amiability, patting my arm as she did so. "It must be so fun for you guys to go out for tacos once in a while."

"I'm sure you get tired of the barbecued pork," Jim said knowingly.

Being mostly a Midwesterner, I'm a patient man, but even a Hoosier can get riled now and then. "Barbara?" I began mildly. "Take a look at Hector over there." I nodded toward our waiter. "And the hostess. And the busboy."

Barbara blinked.

"These people aren't pretending to be Hispanic. They're honest-to-goodness Mexicans."

Barbara looked sympathetically at the staff, then back at me. "Well, I'm sure they try very hard," She said, as if they'd all placed third in a beauty contest.

"Sure," Jim said. "I'm sure the food will be great. Just great."

We sat in silence for a minute or two, trying to ignore a trio of mariachi horns. Hector wandered over with chips and salsa.

"Quiere mild or hot, amigo?"

It was the devil that made me do it.

"Let's have the other stuff, Hector. The house salsa."

"You mean muy caliente?"

"Yeah."

Hector paused. He looked at Jim and Barbara, then disappeared into the kitchen.

I set the napkin dispenser in front of Barbara and smiled. "You're gonna love it," I said. "It's very authentic."

Faux Authentic

My friends had not heard, apparently, that Indianapolis has one of the highest concentrations of Mexican immigrants in the United States. The government of Mexico recently opened a consulate in the city, which now has about as many supermercados as it does Starbucks. El Ranchero may be lowbrow, but it offers real tortillas served up by natives of Mexico.

What could be more real?

Yet authenticity had a different connotation to Jim and Barbara, as it does to most of us. To them, authentic cooking was that which met a subjective standard. It looked Mexican. It was called by Mexican names. It was perhaps based on traditional Mexican dishes. But it was to be found only in upscale restaurants in Southern California—the spiritual home of *real* Mexican cuisine—not in a chartreuse-and-lavender cantina in Indianapolis. And it would not, certainly, come wrapped in a tortilla and smothered with refried beans. To my friends, that which is authentic is that which is tasteful, thoughtfully done, appropriate, haute. Inauthentic is anything gauche, indecorous, or, worst of all, out of date.

Like many Christians, Jim and Barbara take their notion of authenticity to church with them. I've done it too. To them, authentic Christianity is relevant, tasteful, and highly evolved—it's *honest*, for heaven's sake. They consider their church authentic because their pastor preaches in cargo shorts and goes rock climbing on his day off. They themselves are authentic because they are candid about the neglect of their devotional life. It would be inauthentic—phony—to pray when they don't feel like it, so they don't. They are authentic because they deal realistically with issues like abortion, homosexuality, and divorce.

When Barbara mentioned in a previous conversation that she had been divorced and that her children now lived with their father, my wife was sympathetic. "I'm so sorry," Heather offered. "He not only left but took the kids with him?"

"Oh, God no," Barbara said, as if the oath made her denial more believable. "I left *him*. I couldn't stand him preaching at me all the time, using the Bible to beat me down."

Heather, seldom at a loss for words, responded soothingly. "You must have felt so lonely," she said. "I know the Christian community can be judgmental sometimes."

Barbara frowned as if trying to comprehend Heather's meaning. "God no," she said it again. "My church friends have been great. They told me, 'Honey, sometimes you just have to do what you have to do.'"

Barbara acted pragmatically when she ended her bad marriage. Was she being authentic? Was the spiritual advice she received authentically Christian because it displayed tolerance? How are we to know? How do I know that I'm authentically Christian? How do you?

In the world of art, a painting or sculpture that is purported to be the work of someone other than its true maker is called a forgery. There have been some notable examples. In 1496 Michelangelo created his first known sculpture, a sleeping cupid. Because he was unknown as a sculptor, the young artist had little hope of selling his work. So he devised a plan.

Michelangelo buried the marble statue in acidic soil to give it the appearance of being very old. He then sold it to an art dealer who represented it as an ancient Greek objet d'art. The piece was eventually acquired by Cardinal Raffaello Riario of San Giorgio.

But the art was not really ancient, not really Greek, not really—authentic. When the cardinal learned of the forgery, he demanded his money back. Michelangelo was fortunate that the misrepresentation only enhanced his reputation as an artist; some art forgers go to jail.

That which is authentic is that which is objectively verifiable as genuine. An authentic Rembrandt is a painting known to have been created by the artist himself. Authentic Mexican food is that prepared by Mexicans—like the food at El Ranchero. Taste, propriety, suitability for the postmodern world—these are immaterial to the claim of authenticity. What matters is that the item originates from its purported source. That which does so is authentic. Everything else—no matter how relevant—is fake.

What, then, would be an authentic Christian?

TO BE REAL

My wife visited the Netherlands recently, the homeland of both her parents. Heather was raised in the New World but steeped in the Old. Like any good Dutch girl, she attended a

Dutch church, went to a Dutch school, celebrated Dutch holidays, maintained Dutch traditions, and associated mostly with other Dutch children. She is as proud of her Dutch heritage as of her American citizenship. While in Amsterdam, she bought new clothing, delighting in wearing the latest European styles. She immersed herself in Dutch culture. She became finally Dutch, so she thought.

At a grocery store, she waited in line as the clerk finalized a purchase, chatting amiably with her Dutch customer. Then the woman turned to Heather and addressed her in flawless English, "May I help you?"

There is something about being American that cannot be discarded or even disguised. Our nationality is apparent at a glance to both friends and enemies. We cannot conceal our source.

Being a Christian must be the same.

During Jesus' trial, Peter wished to avoid being known as a follower of Christ. He tried everything to dissociate himself from Jesus, but he couldn't. Everything gave him away—his history, his mannerisms, his speech, even his clothing. He had "friend of Jesus" written all over him. He was an authentic Christian, verifiably connected to Jesus himself.

We, on the other hand, try desperately to create the persona of Christ-follower but are often unsuccessful. We name ourselves things like evangelical and fundamentalist. We label ourselves, literally, with bracelets and bumper stickers. We adopt a churchy way of speaking. Yet for the most part, nobody confuses us with friends of God. There are no servant girls persistently accusing us by firelight, "You—you were with him." That may be, quite simply, because we were not. In spite of our claims of authenticity, we have spent very little time with Jesus or none at all. We lack that familiar aspect that can be acquired only by prolonged exposure. There is nothing genuine about our claim to be Christlike, to be Godlike, and everyone knows it but us.

Authentic Christianity is that which originates with Jesus. Authentic Christians are those who associate themselves with him, who know him, who learn from him, who emulate him. Christian identity is not a bracelet or a necklace or a set of lingo. It is a way of being, of thinking, and—most especially—of relating to other people that will be instantly apparent to all who meet us.

This is the authentic Christianity for which I hunger, and it begins with these words: "Blessed are the poor in spirit, for theirs is the kingdom of heaven."

2

vision

"Blessed are the poor in spirit,

Arnie Brinkman was crazy and no mistake. I don't know if he got dropped in the hospital, or slapped around by his parents, or if he was just one of those unfortunate souls born with too few brain cells to power his lightbulb. Either way, he was nuts.

Arnie was in my high school class, or I was in his. As it worked out, I moved just before my senior year at Owosso High School, so Arnie graduated there but I didn't.

I don't tell what's true. I tell what ought to be true.

—BLANCHE DUBOIS IN A STREETCAR NAMED DESIRE

I'm not sure if Arnie ever came to appreciate the irony of the fact that he got to cross the platform at our alma mater while I, who learned so much more there, did not. To me, it became one more clue that the world is a little askew. But as a sixteen-year-old more concerned with making an impression on the improbably gorgeous Angie Dumond than with understanding the moral order, I had no idea why.

But I knew that Arnie was a goof.

Why else would he wear pants that reached barely to the top of his socks—white socks with big blue stripes at the top? And plaid pants. Why else would Arnie wear those glasses, oversized, horn-rimmed bifocals held together by more duct tape than a redneck Christmas present? Why else would Arnie hang around all the smart kids, all the popular kids, and insist that he was one of them when clearly he was not?

Arnie was on the track team, in a manner of speaking. He had no athletic skill, but this was a no-cut sport in which any more-or-less able body was welcome to participate. We kept him around as a mascot. Arnie was tall, about six-one, and he weighed about 114 pounds. His legs were longer than the credits on a feature film, and he had asthma. When he ran, he looked like a stork with an inner ear problem. But Arnie was a firm believer in training. As an early adopter of dietary conditioning, he ate sugar to compensate for his physical limitations. Before a meet, you could see Arnie walking around the locker room with a brown bag filled with the white granules.

He ate it by the handful and always offered to share. "Want some?" he would say. "Makes you fast." Nobody bothered to laugh behind Arnie's back. We laughed to his face. We ridiculed him and belittled him. We called him an idiot.

People did that to Jesus, too. They called him crazy. Even his friends did. They went to collect him one day, thinking that he was "beside himself," meaning, literally, outside his mind. Like Arnie, Jesus had made some improbable statements. He told people, "Whoever eats my flesh and drinks my blood has eternal life." And he said, "Before Abraham was born, I am." Abraham had been dead in the ground for about two thousand years.

Psycho. What else can you say about it?

The statements that Jesus made about himself, though, we might forgive. It's hard for any of us to have a completely accurate picture of ourselves. Doesn't everyone have some fantasy of grandeur? Because we keep them mostly to ourselves, we're considered sane. Jesus had the poor judgment to say these things aloud, which accounts for his friends calling the men in white coats.

But Jesus said things about the world that were just as bizarre. Here's what I'm talking about:

Blessed are the poor in spirit,
for theirs is the kingdom of heaven.
Blessed are those who mourn,
for they will be comforted.

Blessed are the meek,

> for they will inherit the earth.

Blessed are those who hunger and thirst for righteousness,

> for they will be filled.

Blessed are the merciful,

> for they will be shown mercy.

Blessed are the pure in heart,

> for they will see God.

Blessed are the peacemakers,

> for they will be called sons of God.

Blessed are those who are persecuted because of

> righteousness,

> for theirs is the kingdom of heaven.

This is nonsense, of course. It makes less sense than Arnie Brinkman telling people that sugar makes you fast. Poor people are not happy. Nice guys do not finish first. Good losers are still losers, and everybody knows it. So Jesus was crazy. Yet we keep him around as a sort of mascot. We tell stories about him to our children, we invoke his name at weddings, and dedicate gymnasiums in his honor. But nobody takes what he said too seriously. How can we?

Yet maybe he knew something that we don't. Is it possible that he had caught a glimpse of something real, something that none of the rest of us can see? Perhaps, like a dog, he could hear things too high, too pure, for our senses.

Whichever it was—lunacy, plot, or reality—Jesus had a name for this vision. He called it the kingdom of heaven.

ALTernaTe ReaLITY

When confronted with distasteful facts, one lies. Adam stretched the truth when he found himself naked, and naked people have invented their own covering ever since. That's why we have statisticians and lawyers and public relations experts: to imagine for us a better reality than the one that exists.

No class of people is more adept at this kind of obfuscation than are mothers. My own mother is queen among them. For as long as I can remember, she has told the most outrageous tales about her family and especially about her children. In her private vision of reality, my siblings and I are idyllically handsome, incomparably talented, and enviably successful. When my brother got a job with a government contractor, she told people that "senators ask his advice all the time." He answered mail from congressional offices. When my brother-in-law took a job with the attorney general, she told her friends that he was "very high up" in state government. His office was on the twenty-seventh floor. As for me, her son "the writer"? Pinocchio never told such whoppers as my mother has told about me.

My mother is not alone in this; all mothers present an improbably wonderful vision of their children. Can you blame them? Everyone realizes that some things are true but simply shouldn't be. No mother should have a son in prison or addicted to meth or bankrupt or lazy or divorced. But some do. So they lie. It's what people do.

People lie about the world, too, for there are some facts so distasteful, so ugly, that they cannot be accepted at face value. That explains why women continue to live with men who beat them, why children make excuses for their alcoholic parents, and why nobody believes there's a hole in the ozone layer. When we don't like the truth, we invent a reality that feels better.

That makes it difficult to judge most of the things Jesus said about himself and about the world. They have no connection to reality, at least not the one we see. It is not possible to reconcile the fact that one hundred million people were killed by wars in the twentieth century with the belief that God blesses peacemaking. If it is true that God cares for the helpless, then it is impossible that there could be fourteen million AIDS orphans in the world. Those presentations of reality are flatly incompatible. The way Jesus saw the world—this kingdom that he spoke of—and the way the world really is are quite different.

Which is true? Which vision of the world is more reliable? Which is real? And while we're asking, who made the rule that in order for something to be real it has to exist?

On August 28, 1963, Martin Luther King Jr. rallied thousands to the cause of civil rights with his famous words, "I have a dream." King painted a vision of the world in which character matters, color doesn't, and all people are accorded dignity. Nothing could have been further from reality in 1963. Were King's words untrue? Or were they true but unrealized? For four hundred years, scientists and historians have told us that in order for something to be true it must exist in time and space. If you can touch it, they claim, if you can observe it or measure it or objectively verify it, then it is real. Truth is what we experience.

They are wrong.

Poets, artists, and lovers have always known that the truest of all things are those we believe regardless of whether we have experienced them. For by believing them, we cause them to exist. And by acting on that belief, we cause them to appear in time and space. There is a heaven, Jesus taught. You just can't see it. But when you believe it, you make it real, right here, right now. He looked beyond the horizon into a world where the last are first, the cursed are blessed, and those who give their lives away gain the most of all. Nothing could have been further from reality then or now. Yet it was true because Jesus made it true. And when we believe it, it is still true. Jesus was a poet and an artist, not a scientist, and he calls his followers to accept his alternative view of reality and live their lives the same way.

Not surprisingly, few of us are willing to do that.

Between Two Worlds

One of the more distasteful facts that I must constantly face, and therefore constantly obfuscate, is the fact that I call myself a Christian but do not embrace the vision that Jesus had for the world or live by it—at least not often. This kingdom of which he spoke does not describe the world in which I live and work and raise my family. And if I am to be completely honest, I must admit that I don't really want it to. That would require far too much work to bring that about, and I am far too lazy.

For example, I don't hunger and thirst for righteousness. I'd like, in some vague way, to be a better person. But I don't hunger to be rid of anger the way I'm dying for some fries to go with that Coke. And I have very little concern for justice. Sure, I want middle class tax relief (I deserve it) and I want criminals to be incarcerated (they've got it coming). But I don't lose sleep over things like that. I want life to be fair, but I don't thirst for righteousness the way I long for a Gatorade after biking in the sun. Tending to sick people. Creating economic and ecological harmony. Making peace. Being Godlike in the way I think about sex or speak to people or spend money. None of that means anything to me. I'd like the world to be a slightly better place in that I'd like fewer terrorist attacks and more vacation days, but I'm not dissatisfied with my life. I don't have an overwhelming desire to make things right with God and right with other people. At the end of the day, I'm always more concerned about me than about anything else in the universe.

And that's the problem, not with me alone but with everybody. The human heart in all of its manifestations—culture, ideology, political systems—is selfish. The reason things like poverty, genocide, sex slavery, and pollution exist is that we care too much about ourselves and too little about others. And that is what Jesus came to change. He inaugurated an alternative way of looking at life—the kingdom of heaven—in order to turn back to God all that we have turned toward ourselves. This was his vision for the world, and his vision for us. It is his vision for me. So there is no sense in calling myself a follower of Jesus or a fully committed believer or a disciple or any of the other polite names by which Christians identify themselves if I'm not going to deal with this issue of selfishness first in my own heart, then in my relationships, and finally in the culture and systems of the world in which I live. Jesus didn't come to create impotent, docile followers who would mumble a harmless benediction over a depraved world. He came to enlist members of an alternative society, soldiers for a new regime who would wage a war of infiltration on the kingdom of earth.

Here's my problem: I don't know if I'm up for that. Inside of me will always be the reasonable guy who wants to play it safe, take it easy, blend in with the crowd, go along, get along, and prosper. I'd rather live in my nice home, commute to my comfortable office, and snuggle on the couch with my wife than invest my time and energy in trying to right a world that's been broken for a million years.

But that is what Jesus did, and that is what he expects, even demands, of me. I reluctantly agree that I need either to pry the fish sticker off my SUV or begin the hard work of comparing the values I live by with the kingdom of heaven. As things stand, I'm living a double life, trying to maintain dual citizenship both here and in the Kingdom. But that can't last much longer; the seismic tension is too great. Soon the universe will shift and make itself right again, and both feet will land forever in one world or the other.

BOTH FeeT In

It is an embarrassment to me that I called Arnie Brinkman an idiot in high school, because nothing could have been further from the truth. I realized that on the day of the sectional meet at Mount Pleasant, in which I competed in the 110-yard high hurdles. I was a mediocre athlete, but, like Jesus, I had an optimistic vision of what was possible. I wanted to win the sectional and prove to my parents, to my coach, and most of all to Angie Dumond that I was worth something after all. I took my place in lane one, nearest the infield. In the blocks next to me was a kid from archrival Flushing who had legs

like an antelope. I had that nagging feeling again that something might be off-kilter in the universe, but I ignored it. The
gun sounded.

I cleared the first hurdle in stride with the man-deer. At the
second hurdle, I was a half-step off the pace. At the third hurdle, the cosmos shifted. A spike on my left shoe caught the
wooden crossbar. It fell forward, carrying my foot with it. I
sprawled on the track, chin on the tar, foot caught in the hurdle,
blood in my mouth. I was disqualified. Worse, I was humiliated.
I prayed briefly that the world would stand still or that I might
be seriously hurt, even killed, so that I wouldn't have to stand
up and walk off the track a loser. But there was no God. There
was only Arnie, standing in the infield, clapping like a fool,
jerking his head to one side like he always did, and saying,
"That's all right, man. That's all right. Get up, man. You're all
right." He reached out to lift me off the tarmac, and he put his
arm around my shoulder and said it again: "That's all right,
man. You did great." Then he handed me a bag of sugar.

When I think about that day when the world tilted on its
axis, I sometimes recall the words of Jesus, who said that
those who fail in attempting a good thing will be better for
the effort, and that those who help others in their moment of
weakness are blessed above all people—or something like
that. And in those moments, it occurs to me that the world
may not be exactly as it seems and that bringing heaven to
earth might just be possible after all.

My mother, by the way, shameless prevaricator that she is, has lately been telling people that her son the "best-selling" writer is on some short list in New York or Stockholm or somewhere. I don't have the heart to tell her that I'm a hack and that my books are barely noticed by my own publicist. It would break my mother's heart to see her son as he really is. My mother also tells me, every time she sees me, that I'm a great man, a good man, a man who believes in beauty and eternity, who lives by the Spirit, who honors God and truth and family—a man of God. My mother believes this with all of her heart. She makes me believe it too.

This is the power of faith. It is the power to see what is not and by seeing it, to make it real. This is the power that brought light from darkness, order from chaos, something from nothing. This is the power that makes, from hapless, depraved people, children of God. And this is the power that looks at the world and sees justice, equality, mercy, and peace, and in seeing them, causes them to take shape in time and space. This is the kingdom of heaven. This is where I belong.

3

SIGNIFICANCE

"You are the light of the world."

It's easy to make a buck. It's a lot tougher to make a difference.

— TOM BROKAW

Joey Stanley was the hero of my Little League team. This kid was a freak of an eight-year-old, a fifty-two-inch Mickey Mantle with mad skills on the diamond. I once saw him hit four homeruns in a row, and he stole second base about as casually as most kids picked their nose. In place of an arm, he had a Roman catapult that could throw runners out from deep in the hole. Not many kids could hit it deep to short, and none of them could run all that fast. But nobody stood a chance against Joey. Thanks to him, the North Lakeport Tigers were four and zero at the end of June.

I, on the other hand, was the goat of my Little League team. No eight-year-old had a worse aptitude for baseball, which explained why I occupied what is the last place on any baseball roster, right field. Every time a batter swung, I prayed that the ball would go somewhere else. Usually it did, and no pardoned convict was ever more grateful. As a batter, I was more of a barn door. I had kind of a slow, rusty swing, and almost everything flew past me. I reached base only once during the season, on a walk. But Joey? Now there was a ballplayer. In the summer of 1968, I wanted to be just like Joey Stanley.

And perhaps I would have been, given a little more time on the practice field. Unlike Joey, I came from a family of devout Christians, so I was in church about twice as often as I was on the ball diamond. On Sundays, when most of the neighborhood gang was out playing a pickup game, I was indoors, reading Sunday school papers and wishing I could die. Sunday was the Sabbath day, and no ball playing was allowed. On Wednesday nights I went to prayer meeting. Never mind that I prayed even less often than I got a piece of Rod Brown's fastball. Wednesday night was church night, and we never missed.

In the middle of the Little League season, I was forced to take a break from baseball as my family loaded up the Pontiac and headed for camp meeting. I would miss two games. I didn't bother to tell anybody on the team where we were going. How could I explain that I'd be sitting for hours on end on torturous wooden benches in a barn-like tabernacle and listening to three sermons a day while they were out playing baseball like normal people? I didn't even tell the coach. "You going on vacation, Wilson?" he asked me. "Um, sure," I said. There was no way to explain what it meant that my family was Christian.

At least I was home in time for the league tournament. We had suffered only one loss by the end of July, to the Jeddo Cubs. These archrivals would be our first opponent in the playoffs, and we had sworn revenge for the ten-run licking they'd put on us. After practice one Saturday, the coach announced the schedule for the big game. It would be held at 6:00 p.m. on Wednesday. Wednesday was prayer meeting night, and my family never missed.

"Please," I begged, "just this once. I'll be good. I'll clean my room. I'll mow the lawn. I'll do dishes every night until Christmas. *Please* let me skip church and go to the game."

My parents actually wavered, and even that surprised me. For a few minutes, they considered allowing their son to be absent from the Lord's house in order to pursue worldly entertainment. It was a playoff game, after all, and even they could see that playing baseball didn't exactly place me on the road to perdition. But somewhere in the discussion came the mention of my family, meaning my extended family. This great cloud of witnesses, headed by my saintly grandfather and including countless great-aunts and -uncles, most of them preachers, could never, my parents believed, approve of skipping prayer meeting. So on Wednesday, July 24, 1968, I played the first three innings of our game against the Cubs. Then I walked out of the dugout, got in the car, and went to church. When I was eight years old, I knew one thing about what it meant to be a Christian. I knew it meant that you were different from everybody else. And I hated it.

An ODD LOT

If my parents and grandparents and the entire Pilgrim Holiness Church had it in their heads that they should look and act a little different from their neighbors, they at least came by the idea honestly. "For what do righteousness and wickedness have in common?" Paul railed at the Corinthian church. "Or what fellowship can light have with darkness? . . . What does a believer have in common with an unbeliever?" And didn't the great apostle have Isaiah's backing? "Therefore come out from them and be separate, says the Lord. Touch no unclean thing, and I will receive you." How could anybody call himself a Christian and do the things that sinners do? What would John the Baptist have to say about playing ball on Sunday or two-piece bathing suits or Hollywood movies? No sir, we would not take the first step on the slippery slope that leads to destruction, and we had a little ditty to help enforce this mind-set on young people: "We don't drink, and we don't chew, and we don't go with girls that do." Not that we went with girls in the first place.

If we didn't dance or play cards or imbibe intoxicating liquors, we were only doing as the Bible clearly instructs: we were making a distinction between ourselves, the children of light, and the children of darkness all around us. And what was true for my own admittedly conservative branch of the family tree was true of broader Christendom as well. In one way or another, we were different, intentionally different, from the world. We were a prophetic people. But I'd had enough of being different, and I wasn't alone.

On October 11, 1962, Pope John XXIII convened the Second Ecumenical Council of the Vatican, known as Vatican II. The council met four times over the next three years, and although it addressed many areas of church life, it is popularly known for these two: the Roman mass could now be said in the vernacular; and fasting on Fridays, required since A.D. 988, was now merely advised. This meant that Catholics would hear something other than Latin at church, and best of all, could eat something other than fish on Fridays. Catholics were tired of being different.

So were evangelicals.

When I was eight years old, the household names in every evangelical family, what passed for Christian celebrities, were evangelists. Billy Graham was their king, of course, but there were many others. And people still remembered the likes of Billy Sunday—the baseball player turned Bible thumper whose colorful preaching had attracted over one hundred million attendees to evangelistic campaigns in the early twentieth century. He could also run the bases in fourteen seconds, even faster than Joey Stanley. In the 1970s, thousands of would-be soul winners were trained to start spiritual conversations by knocking on doors and asking strangers this painfully direct question: If you died tonight, how certain are you that you would go to heaven?

People really did that.

As a nineteen-year-old college student, nothing sounded more appalling to me. I felt a bit bad that some people might wind up in hell, but not bad enough to walk up to a total stranger and say, "Hello. I'm a religious nut. Would you like to be one too?" I'd rather have told Joey Stanley that I wore girls underpants.

By the time I reached seminary, I heard of a new approach to attracting people to the gospel, one that didn't require me to look like an idiot, again. A new congregation in the Midwest had been formed on the revolutionary notion of making people feel at home in church. This team of evangelists had begun by canvassing their neighborhood, but rather than asking "Are you going to hell tonight?" they asked people "Why don't you like going to church?" Studying their responses, the team formed a congregation that de-emphasized religious language and symbols so that people would feel at ease.

At last, I thought, somebody gets it. People don't want to be different. Christians don't want to be different. Even sinners don't want to be different. This is the great untaught lesson from elementary school, the lesson I could have shared after my baseball summer: *nobody* wants to be different. Everybody wants to fit in. And if we have heroes at all, they're people who are good at something, like playing baseball or making money. Evangelists were passé. As a newly confirmed ordinand, I had a new set of heroes: psychologists, management gurus, and leadership experts. Now, rather than confronting sinners, we would help them understand themselves. In place of evangelistic meetings, we could organize concerts. Instead of skipping baseball to go to church, we would play baseball at church.

Thank God, I wouldn't have to be different anymore.

WE'RE NOT DIFFERENT

It worked. I am today not much different than the non-believers who live all around me. Sure, I once did without television for a few years. I've occasionally railed against the evils of alcohol, and I've protested abortion a time or two. But for the most part, I'm not noticeably different from my neighbors. I have an IRA and a mortgage and a car payment. I wear Old Navy and drink Starbucks and watch football, just like everybody else. I've done so well at blending in with the world that nonbelievers sometimes want to be friends with me, not because they see me as unusual in some way but precisely because they don't. My children, in fact, are surprised at the notion that there might be some practical difference between Christians and Jews and Muslims and run-of-the-mill pagans. "We're all Americans, aren't we?"

My church, like most churches these days, looks and feels exactly like a gym or a concert hall, depending on how the chairs are arranged. Our services are accessible and comfortable and mildly entertaining, like a talk show. There is little, if anything, that would make nonbelievers—what we used to call sinners—feel the least bit uncomfortable. Perhaps that's a good thing. In fact, people who care nothing for God visit our church every Sunday, and when they see how Christians behave around the Holy One of Israel, they usually say things like "That was fun" or "You guys have a cool band."

Jesus said, "You are the salt of the earth. But if the salt loses its saltiness, how can it be made salty again? It is no longer good for anything, except to be thrown out and trampled by men. You are the light of the world. A city on a hill cannot be hidden. Neither do people light a lamp and put it under a bowl. Instead they put it on its stand, and it gives light to everyone in the house. In the same way, let your light shine before men, that they may see your good deeds and praise your Father in heaven."

Here's the point.

We're *supposed* to be different from the world. And that difference is supposed to have a positive effect on the world around us. For centuries, that was true. For all of its failures to be Christlike over the centuries, the historic church did at least cultivate the practice of showing compassion to the poor and distressed. There is a profusion of hospitals, universities, and orphanages named after Christian saints because those Christ-followers gave evidence of their holiness by tending to the sick, educating the masses, and caring for the fatherless and, by so doing, inspired others to follow. I've never seen a hospital named after a Wiccan or a New Ager or a Republican or Democrat. Perhaps there are a few, but for two thousand years it has been Christians who were known for taking in unwanted children and treating lepers and reforming prisons.

Today there are over a million abortions performed in North America and countless more unwanted children born alive around the world. Twenty-five million people have died of the modern plague called AIDS, leaving fourteen million fatherless children. More than two million people are held in our prisons, and thousands more are held captive in our prisons of war. These days, I notice that Christians don't found many hospitals or orphanages or reform movements, but we are quite good at establishing television networks, selling books, raising money, and building gymnasiums. We excel at blocking legislation and electing presidents and dictating public policy. Is this the salt of which Jesus spoke? Is this the light?

Are these the good deeds that will cause others to stand amazed at the glory of God? If we are different as followers of Jesus Christ, it is different from our history and not from the world.

If we become so different from the world that we are withdrawn from it, we hide our light; we do nothing to penetrate the darkness. If we become so much like the world that we blend with it, we have lost our savor; we do not season the world with goodness. Surely there must be a middle way.

LET IT SHINE TILL JESUS COMES

My grandfather, Lawrence W. Wilson, was born in a tiny mining town in the Adirondacks in 1899. His lifetime spanned most of what may have been the most thrilling and tumultuous period in recorded history, the twentieth century. During my grandfather's lifetime, human beings discovered the power of flight and exploited that power all the way to the moon. The automobile was invented and placed into mass production, transforming the shape of restaurants, cities, and even families. Morse code was the only way to communicate over long distances when my grandfather was born. Shortly before he died, *Time* magazine declared the personal computer to be its "man" of the year. During my grandfather's life, Western civilization tried two times to destroy itself. Lawrence W. Wilson lived through an amazing era in the history of the world.

But like me during the summer of 1968, my grandfather was mostly a spectator to the grand achievements of others. The mine that supported the company town in which he was born eventually closed. Grandpa, destined to live in the dirty industrial cities of the Northeast, moved to Rensselaer, just across the Hudson River from Albany. He was too young to serve in World War I and too old for World War II. Besides, he worked in an essential industry. Grandfather had a job in a felt mill, making woolen bedding for the U.S. Army. When all the young men went to Europe, again, to save the world, my grandfather went to work in a blanket factory.

Grandfather went to church every time the doors were open, just as my own dad did, just as I did. Yet if I was peculiar for not playing baseball on Sunday, my grandfather was more so. He wouldn't even watch the sport on the Sabbath. That was the Lord's Day, not to be profaned by worldly entertainment. My grandfather read the Bible a lot, and prayed quite a bit, and I never heard one swear word from his lips, not even after he dropped a limb from his willow tree on the power line. He was different, for sure. Even at church, though, my grandfather was not what you'd call a standout. Some of his brothers were preachers, great leaders in the Holiness Movement that swept the country in wake of the Second Great Awakening. Grandpa was the janitor at his church. It was his job to make sure all the lights were off and doors locked after every service.

My grandfather died in 1985, while I was studying for the ministry. I was reading about people like Dietrich Bonhoeffer and Martin Niemöller, German pastors who had stood up to the Nazis during World War II. These were men who had made a difference in the world. They had risen to the great conflict of their age. They had spoken truth to power, they had taken courageous stands at the risk of their lives, they had achieved the ecclesiastical equivalent of hitting four homeruns in a row. Bonhoeffer was executed and Niemöller imprisoned, all while my grandfather was making blankets in Rensselear. In my family, it seemed, the grandest thing one could do for Christ was to sweep the church floor and not play ball on Sunday.

At my grandfather's funeral, the great cloud of witnesses was gathered—or what was left of it. Most of my great-aunts and -uncles were already dead. The smattering that remained appeared to have been kept in a time capsule—they looked to me exactly as they had in 1968. One person, however, was quite different.

Teddy Parker had been a gangly teenager whenever I'd met him before. I vaguely remembered him from visits to my grandparents' house. He was not quite related to my family, a sort of foster brother to my father. Teddy's parents had worked a lot and asked my grandmother to look after him from time to time. Teddy stayed with them first during the week, when his parents were busy, and then on weekends, when they were drunk. After a while, he stayed all the time. My grandparents had taken this boy into their home and raised him as their own son.

At the graveyard, Teddy came up to me. He came up to all of us, in fact, aunts, uncles, cousins. He wanted to say something about my grandfather. He wanted to say thank you to somebody for what my grandfather had done. Since my grandfather was dead, he said it to all of us. Like Granddad, Teddy didn't say too much. But he said enough. "Your grandfather meant a lot to me," he said, shaking my hand solemnly. "He was a great man."

It occurred to me then that being different from the world is not such a bad thing. Against a landscape of giants—inventors, astronauts, war heroes—my grandfather's life was imperceptible. Yet his godly character, his compassion for others, his gentleness and self-control stood in sharp relief against the violence, dissipation, and hopelessness of the bleak century in which he lived. This is the life of the Christian, the true imitator of Jesus Christ—to be different from the world, and in so doing to have an ameliorating effect on those around us. We long to prosper, to achieve, to be applauded. But Jesus wants for us something quite opposite. Don't be afraid to be different, Jesus tells us, for in so doing, you will save the world.

4

HOLINESS

"Unless your righteousness surpasses
that of the Pharisees . . ."

Albert Harkema was a godly
man, probably the godliest
man in the tiny Michigan town
where I grew up. He was a teacher at the
Christian school and a lifelong member of the
Berean Bible Church. He wore a black suit and tie
every day to school, and every night after supper, he
would gather his family in the living room—his wife,
Elizabeth, and his daughters, Miriam and Esther—and

*An ethical person ought to do more than he's required to do and
less than he's allowed to do.*

—MICHAEL JOSEPHSON

he would read the Bible to them, usually for about an hour. Then they would pray.

The Harkemas did not own a television set, for television was the devil's tool. The Harkema girls, ages eleven and sixteen, always wore skirts below the knee and never appeared in public wearing shorts. They wore one-piece bathing suits, and then only in the company of family, never around boys. Miriam, the elder daughter, was a wholesome beauty, one of the most attractive girls at her school. But she never dated, not even Christian boys. Miriam would remain pure while many other girls, even Christian girls, were falling into sexual sin. Her father would see to that. The Harkema family was present at church every Sunday for both morning and evening services. On Wednesday nights the girls attended the youth group, Elizabeth Harkema taught in the children's club, and Mr. Harkema taught the adult Bible study.

Few people lived a more regimented life than did Albert Harkema. He rose at five o'clock each morning to spend time in prayer and Bible study. He ate sparingly, maintaining his athletic physique at a constant 170 pounds. His hair and fingernails were trimmed fastidiously. Mr. Harkema ran for exercise, and he could be seen three or four times each week jogging resolutely—often sprinting—along the nearly deserted county roads. He covered no fewer than twenty miles each week, and he ran in all weather, eyes fixed in a thousand-yard stare, oblivious to passersby, impervious to pain, equally heedless of the dire heat of summer and the merciless cold of the Michigan winter. He was focused, disciplined, temperate, and self-controlled. Albert Harkema was holy. No one could deny that; indeed, no one ever tried. Everyone in the school where he taught, the church where he worshipped, and the town where he lived understood that this was a righteous man.

Maybe that's why nobody liked him.

UNHOLY THINKING

I have known people like Albert Harkema my whole life and have usually despised them. Angela Davis was the first such person I met, a sniveling, blonde-haired, goodie-two-shoes of a second grader. She turned me in to Mrs. Dwyer for using a bad word on the playground. Angela was so good that she seemed inhuman; she never cheated, never stole, never lied. All the teachers loved her; all the boys hated her. If I could ignore Angela most of the time (a difficult chore since she was my desk mate), I could not ignore the many other Albert Harkemas in my life—kids in the church youth group, Bible teachers at summer camp, old people at my church, classmates in college, missionaries, pastors, saints. Everywhere, it seemed, I was surrounded by people who seemed too good to be true. They did nothing wrong. They were always happy. They read the Bible daily and prayed constantly. And they found it odd that some people who "call themselves Christians" would buy lottery tickets or work on Sunday or take no pleasure in reading 2 Chronicles. These people were holy, and I was nothing like them.

In time I concluded that there was no need to be. The Angela Davises and Albert Harkemas of the world were easy to dismiss as radicals, Pharisees, legalistic snobs who knew nothing of real life. They were so determined to observe the letter of the law that they probably couldn't see the two-by-four in their own eyes—as I was sure Jesus had said somewhere. The standard of holiness they set was so impossibly high that no normal person could achieve it. So as a young adult, I quietly excused myself from the austere, disciplined devotion to God's law that they practiced. I determined that going to church was a right and not a duty, that it was no sin to be tempted nor to flirt with temptation, and that God's grace so freely given was meant to be freely enjoyed. Emboldened by the impossible standard set by the likes of Albert Harkema, I liberated myself from slavish devotion to the law of God.

I was not alone in so doing, and my reaction illustrates one of two classic misinterpretations of the concept of righteousness, which is to conclude that because God is gracious, our behavior is unimportant.

It's not as if we have no scriptural support for this way of thinking. Jesus himself liberalized the observance of the law, to the great disdain of his critics. Jesus healed people and picked grain on the Sabbath, both in violation of the law. He hung out with disreputable people; he didn't wash his hands before dinner; people said he drank too much. Jesus came to start the party, which is why his first miracle was to turn water into wine. In a religious climate where anyone driving two miles an hour over the speed limit was considered a sinner, Jesus said, "Lighten up." The law, apparently, meant nothing to him. Grace was everything.

Paul picked up the drumbeat in his letters, warning the fledgling church to avoid measuring its righteousness by a standard of behavior. Being a Christian isn't a matter of what you eat or drink, he said, or how strictly you reckon your tithe or observe the Sabbath. Where the Spirit of the Lord is, there is freedom.

I heard that. Apparently many others Christians did too, including those who redefine marriage, casually accept divorce, and utterly disregard the Sabbath. We consider God's law to be advisory, at best. Sure, it would be best to avoid profaning the name of the Most High God, but it's not as if he'll put you in hell for it.

Resolute in our conviction that "nobody's perfect" and that God permits, even expects, us to sin every day in thought, word, and deed, we define righteousness as a healthy dependence on grace. The result is a lazy religion that not so much embraces sin as fails to notice it. We're not amoral people. We're just not perfect. What could be wrong with that?

The problem with this way of reckoning righteousness is that it makes the most sinful person out to be the most holy. God is a God of grace, so those who depend most freely on that grace must be the most in tune with his Spirit. Homosexuals are perceived as somehow more holy than "homophobes" because they understand that God is accepting. Christians who occasionally drink alcohol to excess are more spiritual than teetotalers because they understand the concept of freedom. Believers who fail constantly in observing God's law, confessing every week to their small group, that yes, they lusted, burst into anger, or gossiped yet again, are venerated as the most spiritual members of the group because they are the most honest about who they really are. Should we continue to sin that grace may abound? Yes, by all means, let's do.

False Righteousness

Albert Harkema and his family disappeared from my radar screen sometime during my high school years. I occasionally thought of Esther, who'd been in my grade in school, and Miriam, the stunning beauty. Years after moving away from Michigan, I heard that their father had died of cancer. I remembered the austere man with a mixture of guilt and disdain. As much as I disliked him, I could not escape the feeling that he was somehow the better person. However my holiness might have compared to that of my peers or even of Jesus Christ, I knew that I was nothing at all like Albert Harkema. I now thank God for that, because I know the rest of the sad story of this pitifully broken man.

Albert Harkema had not died of cancer but of AIDS, a secret his family carefully kept for many years. They preserved the myth that this husband and father had been as righteous as he'd appeared to be, concealing the fact that he'd been a closet homosexual, engaging in promiscuous behavior all the while he taught Bible classes and led worship. But the secret unraveled when Esther, the younger daughter, brought forth the even more terrible truth that their father had also been a child molester and that she had been his repeated victim. At first, few people believed it. In time, however, Miriam's bulimia and Esther's promiscuity and drug abuse lent credibility to the claim that there had been something terribly wrong in the Harkema family. Albert Harkema had appeared so perfect, so holy. Yet he was human after all and didn't come close to achieving the standard of righteousness for which he was known.

If my youthful disdain for the law illustrates one mistaken view of holiness, the fall of Albert Harkema tragically illuminates another. For embracing the law is no more a path to holiness than is rejecting it. To say that our behavior is unimportant to God is quite wrong. To say that it is all-important is equally wrong and just as dangerous.

Albert Harkema was a Pharisee, and all Pharisees define holiness as strict adherence to a code of behavior. To the legalist, holiness is not a matter of relying on grace; it is a matter of exercising personal discipline. If those who revel in grace march under a banner that reads "Nobody's Perfect," Pharisees adopt the motto "Just Do It." They, too, have scriptural support. The Bible is clear about what ought not to be done, isn't it? We have ten solid commandments and lots of other imperatives, don't we? Does anybody not know that it's wrong to commit adultery or cheat on your taxes or tell lies? Everyone knows how we ought to live; righteous people are those who do it. Any questions?

The problem with Pharisaism is opposite that of licentiousness in that it ignores not the exterior but the interior life. Those who revel in grace are open in dealing with their inner selves—they freely confess their thoughts, emotions, temptations. Their behavior is the problem. Pharisees are good at behaving well but ignore the interior life that will eventually be expressed in action. While they appear to comply with God's every desire, they may be very different on the inside, as was Albert Harkema. Jesus encountered his share of Pharisees, and he despised their hypocritical insistence that behavior alone was the standard for righteousness.

He called them whitewashed tombs. For Jesus knew what Albert Harkema and so many others have proven: that interior life inevitably spills into behavior. Those who attempt to obey the law but do not truly wish to please God may succeed in complying with little things like tithing and Sabbath observance, but they will most likely fail in even greater, more destructive ways. No hidden thing remains hidden forever. It will out in the end. And that includes hidden sin.

What, then, is true righteousness? If being holy is neither a matter of covering failure with grace nor creating obedience by force of will, what is it?

TRUe RIGHTeousness

Jesus said, "Do not think that I have come to abolish the Law or the Prophets; I have not come to abolish them but to fulfill them. I tell you the truth, until heaven and earth disappear, not the smallest letter, not the least stroke of a pen, will by any means disappear from the Law until everything is accomplished." Jesus is not alone in his respect for God's Word. The psalm writer praised God's law as a source of wisdom: "Your statutes are my delight; they are my counselors. . . . Your word is a lamp to my feet and a light for my path." Moses, David, Paul, Solomon: each of them knew the value of God's revelation, including the Law, which shows us how to live.

As for the standard of righteousness, Jesus went on to say, "For I tell you that unless your righteousness surpasses that of the Pharisees and the teachers of the law, you will certainly not enter the kingdom of heaven." So much for my easy dismissal of Angela Davis, and the legion of Pharisees I have known.

Yet the story of Albert Harkema gives warning that the law is not a savior. Indeed, as Paul said, nobody is made righteous by observing the law. That's because the law can't make you something you're not. It can only reveal what you already are. The law, after all, is not a list of rules. It is a way of being that finds its expression in behavior. To be a safe driver is not to drive exactly the posted speed limit in all situations. It is to operate one's vehicle in such a way that the lives and property of others are protected. Generally, that means observing posted speed limits, but that's hardly the point. Respect for others is the real issue. Those who have it will seldom, though perhaps occasionally, drive faster than the posted limit. That could be why Jesus seemed to be so unconcerned about minor matters of the law that were such sticking points with his critics. He didn't worry about obeying the law because he embodied the law: he was the law. He was the Word of God made into a human being. Jesus behaved, as we all do, in accordance with his true nature. How could he, the living Word, behave unlawfully?

We define righteousness as a matter either of obedience (I'm righteous because I behave well) or of grace (I'm righteous because God loves me). It is neither. We become righteous not when God loves us (he already does) or when we behave well (impossible, as a matter of human willpower) but when we love God. It is then that our exterior life will match our interior life. No one can act indefinitely in some way contrary to his nature. When our interior life is like Jesus' was—wholly devoted to the Father—we will behave accordingly. We will be righteous not merely in name but in fact. This is what Jeremiah saw when he peered into the future, speaking some six hundred years before the time of Christ.

Listen.

"The time is coming," declares the LORD, "when I will make a new covenant with the house of Israel and with the house of Judah. It will not be like the covenant I made with their forefathers when I took them by the hand to lead them out of Egypt, because they broke my covenant, though I was a husband to them," declares the LORD.

"This is the covenant I will make with the house of Israel after that time," declares the LORD. "I will put my law in their minds and write it on their hearts. I will be their God, and they will be my people."

Jeremiah foresaw the day when people would not need law books and rules and traffic cops. They would love God with their whole heart and soul and strength. And when they did, sin would disappear from the equation between God and man. It would be gone, forgotten. Who are the true children of God? Who is holy? Who is righteous in his sight? Those whose hearts are wholly devoted to God. Do they obey the law? Are they holy?

How could they be otherwise?

Heart Holiness

God did not do a bad thing when he gave us the law. He gave us a guide for living, ten infallible rules for living a healthy, happy life. It has been our practice to use those rules as clubs with which to beat others or as distorted mirrors with which to prove our own righteousness, something God never intended. And God did not do a bad thing when he freely forgave our sins. It is our practice to use God's grace as a cover for our sin, abusing the freedom that he has given us. Jesus showed us a different way.

In our culture there is a custom which holds that men shall honor their wives on their birthdays. Countless chick flicks, florists, and greeting card companies reinforce this behavior. It is something like a law in our society. My wife's birthday is April 4, and I always comply. If I were to forget my wife's birthday, I might expect to be punished in some way—at least by a little ribbing from my workmates. How many flowers are purchased each year based on the fear of offending a spouse? Is this obedience? Is it love?

Yet I have no fear of offending Heather. She has never demanded that I show her respect, and I have no fear that she would be insulted if I forgot her birthday. It may be true that remembering my wife's birthday is in some sense the right thing to do. But that's not why I do it. I honor Heather because I love her. I buy her flowers or a card or a gift because I delight in her and enjoy demonstrating that to her. She rewards me simply by being delighted in return. I suspect she knows that I buy the flowers at the grocery store and always choose the least expensive card, yet she gushes over these trinkets as if they were extraordinary. It isn't the gift itself that matters to her; it is the fact that I love her that brings her pleasure. I delight in her, and she delights in me. There is little chance that I will give offense or that she would take it if I did. In our relationship there is first love, then honor, and finally grace.

Is there some chance that I can apply this standard to my relationship with God? Could it be that I could come to love God so fully that I would honor him completely? Could I focus so completely on him that I would look beyond the law, immeasurably exceeding that miserly description of obedience? Could it be that my righteousness might somehow exceed that of even the most scrupulous law abider? Could I, who have had such difficulty applying the concepts of obedience and righteousness and holiness come to embody those very ideals not by discipline or force of will but by a love so complete and so animated that it becomes alive in me? Could I choose to do things that honor God not because I must but because I want to?

Jesus said, "The time is coming—and now is—when the true worshipers will worship the Father in spirit and truth."

That time is now, today. Let it be so for me.

5

PURITY

"If your right eye causes you
to sin, gouge it out. . . ."

People so rarely responded to
altar calls when I was a pastor
that I all but quit giving them. Once
in a while I would invite people to come to the
altar and pray following a Sunday morning
sermon, but it was mostly a matter of waving the
flag—standing with every head bowed and every
eye closed as a way of showing that we really do
believe in the convicting power of the Holy Spirit.

Purity and simplicity are the two wings with which man soars above the earth and all temporary nature.

—THOMAS À KEMPIS

I didn't expect anyone to respond. So I was more or less dumbfounded when Mel Farley stepped out from his pew one Sunday on the very first verse of "Just As I Am" and walked resolutely to the front of the church.

We had a seeker.

Mel was an insurance broker and the most convincing salesman I have ever known. When he read the phone book, it made you want to call somebody. Everything about him was inviting. His smile was always present but never forced. His manner was comfortable but not overly familiar. His handshake was just firm enough to be masculine without being overbearing. And although his train stopped well shy of Handsome Station, women seemed to love the guy. He was successful in business, had a lovely family, and was universally admired by people at church. What on earth was he doing at the altar? I couldn't think of a sin Mel was likely to commit—not that I'd ever given it much thought. He was too nice a guy.

My curiosity was sated about three seconds after the benediction, when Elmer Bowles and I gathered around Mel for prayer. I laid a hand on his shoulder and muttered something pastoral like "Brother, how can I pray for you?" Mel got straight to the point.

"It's my marriage, Preacher. It's falling apart."

I wasn't used to such candor, especially in church. I scanned my hard drive for an appropriate response, but Mel pressed on without one.

"You can't wind up right when you start out wrong," he continued, as if reciting a country song. "Roseanne and I started out wrong, and I think that's how we're going to finish."

Still no help from my fading memory of pastoral counseling class. I said, "Umm."

"We wrecked a perfectly good marriage," Mel went on, as sincerely as I've ever heard him speak. "There was nothing wrong with my first wife. I just got bored, I guess."

"Umm."

Mel continued for about five minutes, recounting the details that had led to his trip down the sawdust trail. He and Roseanne had committed adultery during his first marriage and her second. They got married like Johnny and June, in fever, which had lasted for about two years. Now the fire was out. Roseanne lived with remorse over the affair and the nagging feeling that her marital relations with Mel constituted a form of adultery. She was frigid and depressed. Mel lived with Roseanne and the dysfunctional children from her two prior marriages, plus an advanced case of sexual frustration. His salesman charm was completely absent now. He spoke evenly and sincerely, repenting of his adultery and forlornly accepting his situation. It was impossible not to sympathize with this contrite soul.

Mel had begun the interview with candor, and he intended to finish it in the same fashion. "Preacher," he said,

"I don't like the thought of a second divorce. But I'm forty-two years old, and I have needs. I'd just feel better about it if Roseanne and I could stay together and make this thing work. Pray for me, would you?"

I did so immediately.

Can't Stop Thinking About It

The entangled case of Mel Farley presented a dilemma for me as a pastor—and as a Christian. On the one hand, I knew that adultery is sin and that, by Jesus' counsel, divorce and subsequent marriage without proper grounds is likewise sinful. Yet I genuinely sympathized with Mel, who was as contrite over his former sin as he was resolved to sin again if need be. While the preacher inside me was screaming, *Get a grip, pal! You're actually planning to commit adultery,* the realist who so often competes for my attention was completely sympathetic. *I get it, Mel. Self-control only goes so far.*

Human beings are sexual creatures. The drive within us to procreate is as basic and strong—sometimes stronger—than the urge to eat and drink. Corrupted by the Fall, as all of our natural urges have been, the sex drive now propels human beings toward every bizarre behavior from adultery to homosexuality to sadomasochism. Whether rightly directed or not, sex is one of the most basic human desires. So the question for most people is not whether they will have sexual temptations of one kind or another but how they will deal with them. Mel's response captures exactly the man-in-the-pew (and woman-in-the-pew) attitude about sex: it's going to happen, one way or another. Maybe that's why there's a study released every year or so telling us what we already know about Christians and sex, namely that they have just as much of it as anybody else. If the polls are to be believed, Christians have premarital sex, extramarital sex, and homosexual sex just as frequently as do nonbelievers. Our daughters are about as likely to bear children out of wedlock as anybody else's. We divorce just as often as our nonbelieving neighbors. Maintaining sexual fidelity—especially when it involves chastity—seems unrealistic to most people, even to many Christians. Some don't even try.

Overreaction against sexual immorality appears to be an equally unhelpful way of dealing with sexual temptation. Telling a teenager not to think about sex is like telling an eight-year-old not to put a bean up his nose. The admonition virtually guarantees the result. If Mel was guilty for being more concerned about his sexual fulfillment than with the effect of his behavior on others, his wife also bore some responsibility for the sad state of their marriage. Her neurotic concern that having sex with her husband might somehow displease God seemed to be at the root of her depression and her husband's dissatisfaction. Many well-meaning people have missed the joy God intended for married lovers and caused themselves unnecessary guilt and frustration by treating sex—rather than sexual infidelity—as a problem.

The real problem is that we harm ourselves and others when we misuse sex. We alternately see it as a guarantee of fulfillment, pleasure, and intimacy or else a dirty, sordid activity to be undertaken furtively and renounced quickly. As alcoholics with a drop of the grape, we can see no middle way. We will either gratify our desires and the devil may care, or else we will grudgingly, dutifully, painfully bind ourselves to what we judge to be an arbitrary and unfair standard—sex only between heterosexual married partners.

Who can live this way?

You can, according to Jesus. And you must, even if it kills you. Sexual integrity is that important.

TOO IMPORTANT TO IGNORE

Jesus seldom spoke more candidly than he did on the subject of sex. His instructions are clear, direct, and impossible to mistake. If you fantasize about having sex with another person, you've already been unfaithful to your partner. If you act on that wish, you're in danger of hell. If you can't seem to keep your mind right, do something—*anything*—to get control of your thoughts, which dictate your eventual actions. The first step toward doing that is to be honest about sex, something that hasn't come naturally to any human being since, well, ever.

Schadenfreude is not a word that most people would know, in spite of the fact that it's in most English dictionaries. Yet it is a concept with which we are familiar. I imagine it as a championship-caliber word at the Scripps National Spelling Bee. *Derivation?* A combination of German words meaning damage and joy. *May I have a definition?* Enjoyment obtained from the troubles of others. *Please use it in a sentence.* The national schadenfreude was aroused but not nearly satisfied by the moral failure of yet another televangelist.

It is not the sex, it's the lying about sex that really bothers people. This is what countless politicians and not a few Christian leaders have discovered: people will forgive just about any indiscretion if you confess and say you're sorry, but they can't stand a liar. Hypocrisy is the one unpardonable sin in our culture.

Jesus, too, was unfazed by the various sexual expressions that he encountered, including the woman caught in adultery, the sinful woman (perhaps a prostitute) who anointed his feet, and the serial monogamy of the Samaritan woman. He was willing to forgive any sin, and he was realistic about the reasons people divorce. Sex itself was not a problem to Jesus. What he hated was hypocrisy. Hypocrisy flourishes in an atmosphere of secrecy, and we are never more secret than when dealing with sex. Consider the following statements: "Sex is important to me, and I'm angry because my needs aren't being met"; "I think about sex a lot"; "Pornography fascinates me, but I don't want my husband to know"; "I have sexual thoughts about people of the same sex, and I don't know what to do about it." Christians seldom admit these things to themselves, let alone others. So the first step to sexual fidelity may be sexual honesty. Am I willing to be honest with myself about who I am, what I have done, and what I am in fact doing? Do I hide my behavior from others and even deny to myself that I engage in it? Those who have a hard time stating clear answers to these questions will find it impossible to live up to Jesus' high expectation of sexual integrity.

It ought to go without saying but probably doesn't that the object of one's sexual fantasies is not the person with whom to be brutally honest about sex. Confessing your sexual fascination with your boss to your boss is a better way to start an affair than to preempt one.

If Jesus hated hypocrisy about sex, he equally despised the casual acceptance of sexual practices that caused unthinkable harm to others. Can we forget his scathing pronouncement that it would be better to be tossed into the ocean with a millstone around one's neck than to cause a child to sin? Can we perhaps hear an echo of that harangue in Jesus' well-known teaching against casual divorce: If you divorce a woman for no good reason, you cause *her* to commit adultery? Few of us consider the effect of our sexuality upon others. Where is the harm in pornography or prostitution or casual sex? It is the harm caused by treating another person as a thing, an object having no intrinsic value. Misused sexuality dehumanizes people. Therefore, the second step toward living as Jesus lived with regard to sexuality is to consider other people as more important than ourselves—something that should be second nature to a follower of Jesus Christ but too often is not.

Eventually, transparency and humility in the area of sexuality must be translated into action. If you believe that it is important to honor Jesus' teaching concerning sex, you'll have to do something—perhaps something drastic—to make that happen. If lust is a problem for you, Jesus advised, gouge out your eyes. Do whatever it takes to keep your mind on your own wife—sexual fidelity is that important. To what lengths are you willing to go to ensure that your sexual thoughts and behaviors are proper and respectful of others? Would you rip the cable out of your home and live without television or Internet access to avoid being ensnared by pornography? Would you find another job in order to put an end to your lustful thoughts about a coworker? Would you separate yourself from your family to ensure that you will not act on your desire to abuse your own children? Will you find an answer to the difficult question faced by Mel Farley: Am I willing to go without sex rather than harm others? Too often we blame someone else for our failure to maintain sexual integrity. We sin because others place opportunity before us. Sexual images pervade our culture. Pornographers bombard us with solicitations. Women dress provocatively.

So what?

Guarding your integrity is not up to the president or the Screen Actors Guild or your assistant with the short skirt. It's your responsibility to keep your sexual life in order.

This is not rocket science, according to Jesus. Sex can be either a fulfilling, refreshing, affirming experience for two married people—or it can be total hell, a vapid, dehumanizing charade of artificial intimacy and false pleasure. Christians do whatever it takes to prevent themselves from victimizing themselves and others in that way. If that means telling the truth that nobody wants to hear, they do it. If it means sacrificing their own desires in order to protect others, they do it. There's too much at stake to take this lightly.

SO GOOD

Mel and Roseanne stayed married. Mel's hypothesis—that he must have sex with someone besides his wife or else be frustrated—proved to be a false dilemma after all. The two agreed to see a counselor. He, apparently, learned to practice self-control, which is one of the fruit of the Spirit, one mark of an authentic believer. Roseanne finally put her narcissistic twenty-four-year-old son out of the house and insisted that her nineteen-year-old daughter get a job—two steps toward a healthier sex life for the real adults in the house. And she, under the counsel of another pastor, was able to reconcile herself to the less-than-ideal but not sinful state of her marriage to Mel. With prayer and patience and a little help from friends, the two were reconciled. A healthy attitude toward sex goes a long way toward creating a fulfilling life.

Hoping to impart that lesson to the next generation of Christian soldiers, my wife volunteers to conduct sex education with junior high school students. I can't imagine agreeing to be locked in a room with two dozen seventh graders for a whole hour, especially talking about sex. Yet Heather does this willingly. Attacked in her own home by a stranger, Heather faced the double trauma of rape and unwanted pregnancy. In her best-selling memoir, *Startling Beauty*, She wrote about her decision to both accept and love the child produced by that rape—a charming daughter named Rachael. Because of her experience, Heather understands the trauma misused sexuality can produce better than most people do. She accepts her assignment cheerfully, passionately.

A recent abstinence lesson began with the predictably coarse jokes that middle schoolers are prone to make. "I can't wait for this class," one boy said, laughing. "I've got herpes, and my girlfriend's pregnant." The class tittered. "Your girlfriend's not pregnant," a girl retorted. "You're not man enough to get the job done." Heather quickly called the class to order. A pretest of the students showed that their true feelings about sex were little different than their blustering jibes. Of twenty-three students, only one stated that she intended to reserve sex for marriage. Most scoffed at the idea. Nearly half admitted to having had at least one sexual encounter.

Sex is a fact of life for children, too.

Over the five days on which her teaching occurred, Heather used a familiar but effective object lesson. Asking for a volunteer, she placed a piece of duct tape on the student's arm. It was the same boy who'd said his girlfriend was pregnant. "Having sex with someone," she said, "works like duct tape. It sticks you to them. And that's what it's supposed to do."

Heads nodded. They'd seen duct tape before, and nearly half of them already understood that sex is also a powerful bonding agent.

"What happens when you take the tape off?" Heather asked. They all knew. The boy screeched as she snatched the tape from his forearm. "It hurts even more to pull apart two people who have been joined together," she said.

"Will this tape stick again?" Heather asked.

"Yeah, but not as good," someone answered. And she was right. Heather applied the tape several more times to various students, and sure enough, it eventually lost its power to bond.

"That's the way sex is," Heather told them. "If you have sex with many different people, it really won't join you together. But that's not the worst part—look here." She held up the underside of the tape, now covered with hair and dirt.

"Eeew!" the class howled in unison.

"That's what happens when you have sex with lots of different partners," Heather said. "It leaves a real mess behind in your life. It makes you feel awful."

The post-test was unanimous. All twenty-three students emphatically stated that they would cherish the gift of sex and reserve it for their marriage partner.

It still amazes me to hear children speak so openly about sex—and to hear my wife speak just as candidly with them. Yet these kids are little different than Mel Farley or many of us. They are utilitarian in their thinking about sex and oblivious to the damage caused by such carelessness. Thankfully, the words of Jesus have powerful effect, even on such as these.

"I'm going to wait until I'm married to have sex," wrote one twelve-year-old on his course evaluation. "I want sex bad, but I want it to be good."

Out of the mouths of babes.

9
Forbearance

"If someone strikes you on the
right cheek, turn to him the other also."

try to avoid being a jerk; I'm not always successful. Such was the case one rainy day as I made my way home from the shooting range. Some may find it odd that a Christian, a preacher no less, would make a hobby of using firearms. It simply never occurred to me that there could be anything wrong with blasting holes in pieces of paper, or even with hunting. Didn't the Lord tell Peter to "kill and eat"?

It is better to be violent, if there is violence in our hearts, than to put on the cloak of nonviolence to cover impotence.

—Mahatma Gandhi

Pointing a gun at a human being is the last thing I would ever want to do.

The Midwest is cruelly dismal in winter, not so much cold as bleak, and as I drove along the rain-splattered highway, my frame of mind was well matched by overcast sky. I drifted along in a fog not unlike the spray that enveloped my vehicle. I confess that I little noticed the cars around me, and cared even less about who drove them or where they might be going.

Slow driving is a special torture for a purpose-driven soul such as I, especially on a rainy day. For a mile or two, I found myself trapped behind an obstinate semi. I looked for a place to pass. Then I fiddled with my iPod. Then I took a phone call. Finally, I saw a chance to get around the putz. I pulled into the left lane and sped past the truck. A pickup appeared behind me. The driver flashed his lights, as if signaling to yield the road. I got around the semi and pulled back into the right lane. The pickup darted in behind me. The driver pulled up close, so close that his headlights disappeared from view. *Odd,* I thought, *What's this guy up to?* I glanced in the rearview mirror. The guy gave me the finger.

Idiot, I thought, and drove on.

But the pickup followed me. It tailed me into town, a distance of about three miles. I parked on the street to run an errand, and the vehicle pulled alongside and paused. The driver stared at me, face flushed. He gestured more violently than before, and drove on. I got out of my car to enter a drugstore, thinking the incident was over. Meanwhile, the other driver had parked a few spaces ahead. He leapt from his vehicle and ran toward me, screaming.

"You almost killed me!"

"What are you talking about?" I said, trying to keep calm.

"You pulled in front of me, you stupid -----! You almost ran me off the road!" He was within feet of me now, veins bulging from his neck.

Was this road rage?

"Dude, I never saw you," I said, trying to diffuse the tension.

He screamed profanity.

"Hey, man," I said, still hoping to avoid a problem, "I really didn't see you."

"---- you!" Then he spit on me.

Yes, this was road rage. *Loser!* I thought. *Getting in my face. For what? Because I forgot to signal?* This animal had spit on me. *He* spit *on me!* Then it dawned on me. *Larry, you've just been to the range. You've got a .45 right there in the car. It's loaded. You don't have to take this from anybody.*

I stood in silence, shaking inside, inches away from a raging fool in one direction and a loaded pistol in the other. One of us would make the next move.

A Broken Sense of Justice

This is how we are made, or else how we are broken: our basic instinct is to return evil for evil. Everything in our being calls for retaliation when wronged. This is the shattered image of God's justice within us, damaged by the Fall. Our basic instinct to preserve order and fairness becomes an urge to harm others as they have harmed us—or worse. That makes Jesus' teaching on nonviolence extremely difficult for most people to accept. It seems to contradict what we believe to be our best and noblest desires—to seek justice, to redress wrongs, to punish evil. Are we wrong to want wrongdoers brought to justice? Is law enforcement a bad thing? Should we turn aside while wicked people commit wicked acts? Is that what it means to turn the other cheek? Retaliation feels to us like justice, so it's difficult to believe that it's not the right thing to do.

Our culture is even less help than usual at this point. Western democracies are founded on the notion that justice is a higher principle than even law. When a government is unjust, we have been taught, it must be overthrown. Shouldn't this principle apply to personal relationships? A bad marriage is not to be endured. A personal wrong is not to be tolerated. Our movie good guys are all strongmen, teaching us this basic lesson of right and wrong: A man's gotta do what a man's gotta do. When somebody does you wrong, you must take personal vengeance. It's the law of Hollywood.

Even Christian leaders can be blind at this point, viewing the exercise of power, even brutality, as synonymous with righteousness. While returning from a trip one evening, I stood in line at the airport to make a claim for lost luggage. The traveler ahead of me was leading a group of Christian teens who had returned from a missions trip. When told that their luggage would not arrive until the following day, the youth leader had the proverbial cow, raising his voice, making demands, and threatening to file a grievance with everyone from God to the governor of Indiana. "Here's what you're gonna do, sport," he told the beleaguered baggage attendant. "You're gonna deliver our bags to this address by noon tomorrow, or your boss *will* hear about it." I didn't bother to tell the boor that airlines almost always do exactly that when luggage is delayed. Sadly, his outburst seemed to raise, not lower, his esteem in the eyes of the young people to whom he was the chief exemplar of Jesus Christ.

We cannot believe that Jesus' teaching on this point could be accurate, so we reject it out of hand. Surely Jesus doesn't expect you to sit there and smile while your mother-in-law belittles your cooking. Turn the other cheek? It sounds poetic and all that, but it simply isn't practical. Life doesn't work that way. We love the image of Jesus as the firebrand, turning the tables, righting the wrongs. We hear it echoed in political speeches, warmongering sermons, and strident calls for the death penalty. Debauchery, gluttony, drunkenness—we know these things to be wrong even as we engage in them. Afterward, we have the good sense to feel guilty. But vengeance? This actually feels right.

Revenge and retaliation are wolves in sheep's clothing. Feeding on our misplaced sense of justice, they fuel the worst instincts that we have—to hate, to segregate, to destroy.

A Higher Way

The highest award for valor in the United States is the Medal of Honor, which is awarded by the president for acts of bravery that go above and beyond the call of duty, risking one's life in the face of the enemy. Many recipients are given the award posthumously because they died while committing the brave act for which they are honored. We prize self-sacrifice above wealth or fame or any achievement. Everyone knows this. Our greatest respect is reserved for those who sacrifice their lives, not those who mete revenge upon others. Jesus himself is our greatest example, surrendering his life for us all. In spite of the cultural and even religious defenses we make for seeking retaliation, everyone realizes that to surrender one's right is the more noble—the more Christlike—way.

Yet that leaves well-meaning people with a practical question. Are we to retreat meekly whenever challenged by brutish behavior? Are we not to defend helpless people? What does it mean to turn the other cheek?

It may mean, first, that we avoid conflict in the first place. Paul told the Christians at Rome, "If it is possible, as far as it depends on you, live at peace with everyone." In other words, go out of your way to avoid conflict. The book of Hebrews echoes that command: "Make every effort to live at peace with all men and to be holy." The easiest way to eliminate an enemy is to not make one in the first place. Certainly, followers of Jesus Christ ought to be known as people who are generally easy to get along with. Oddly, Christians seem to have acquired the opposite reputation in our culture. We are seen as strident, unyielding, judgmental, and difficult to get along with. Is it possible that we have confused righteousness with priggishness?

Jesus' teaching on nonresistance might be obeyed also by taking the initiative to resolve conflict quickly. If you're on your way to church, Jesus said, and you remember that somebody has something against you, go settle the matter. Don't place even worship ahead of the need to be at peace with others. More often we go on ahead to church and there pray for the damnation of our enemies. Jesus was unconcerned about who held the grievance (you or your neighbor) or about who was in the right. The point was to make peace quickly. Take the initiative to resolve the matter, regardless of who is at fault. How many conflicts between people—and nations— have escalated to the point of violence because one party or the other was unwilling to negotiate a settlement?

A third way of practicing nonviolence is to accept personal injustice in order to preserve peace. During the 1988 presidential election, Michael Dukakis was asked during a debate to defend his opposition to the death penalty. Suppose that someone attacked and killed your wife, the questioner asked. Would you still oppose the death penalty? Dukakis dispassionately stated that he would oppose capital punishment regardless of how it might affect him personally. Nobody believed him. He lost the election.

Like the questioner in that debate, most who argue nonviolence push the discussion to its logical extreme. Would you stand by and allow someone to rape your wife? Does this mean we should tolerate genocide? Would you really allow someone to beat you without fighting back? Such inflammatory questions generally produce the same result they did during the aforementioned presidential debate: they derail the discussion, excusing people from applying the principle of nonretaliation to the more usual disputes they face in life—between neighbors, coworkers, and friends. What do you do when someone cuts you off in traffic? Give him the finger? Spit on him? Shoot him? How do you respond when a coworker takes credit for your idea? Out her to the boss? Gossip behind her back? Sabotage her project by procrastination? Accept personal injustice, Jesus said, in order to keep the peace. Turn the other cheek and move on.

But what about more serious problems such as robbery, violence, or war? I have had the opportunity to visit with

Christians who lived through a particularly brutal civil war in their homeland. During the conflict, rebel soldiers would stop people who were traveling to the market for food and demand half of their money. On their return, the rebels would demand half of their produce. Those who objected were shot. Rebels entered the village where a man called Samuel Johnson lived and demanded that he bring them food. He provided a meal for them. They demanded more. "Bring us food or we'll beat you," they said. He gave them more. They demanded still more food, and Johnson's wife objected. "You're giving these vermin all that we have," she said. "Our children will starve." In her anger, she wanted to curse them—regardless of the consequences.

"No," Samuel said. "Let's give them what they ask."

Weeks later, Samuel and his family were forced to flee from their village because of the fighting. In this conflict that played out largely along ethnic lines, they were in great danger as they traveled. As they neared a rebel checkpoint, they heard gunfire. Some of those passing through, they knew, were being executed. Yet as Samuel and his family approached, they were waved past. "I remember you," said one rebel. "We stopped at your house, and you fed us."

What would I do if my home were threatened? If my children were in danger? If my own life were threatened? I can't imagine how I could remain emotionlessly attached to my principles. But after meeting Samuel Johnson, hearing his story, and seeing the look of contentment on his face in spite of what he had suffered, I have reason to hope that I could. There is no profit in retaliation. As it has been said, an eye for an eye leaves the world half-blind. Our only hope for peace—in the world, in the neighborhood, or in our homes—is to learn to accept personal injustice for the sake of the greater good.

Nowhere, by the way, does Jesus advise anyone to stand by while children are abused or women raped or the helpless mistreated. Jesus surrendered his own life, yet he defended the rights of others. When tempted to use force in any situation, we might first ask this question: will this action protect others or merely avenge myself? Perhaps that should be the test of our willingness to use violence in any situation.

DIM THE LIGHTS

I thank God that the driver of the pickup truck on that rainy day turned on his heel and walked away. I've never seen him since. Violence has never been my tool for resolving conflict, and I use firearms for sport not personal protection. I have little fear that the conflict would have escalated further than it already had. Even so, the thought of retaliation did enter my mind. I spent the rest of the day deeply shaken, both from being angrily confronted and from realizing how easily my own blood can boil. How odd it is that the most basic thing we do each day—drive to work—can place us in line for violent conflict. Martin Luther King Jr., a great apostle of nonviolence, once commented on this very phenomenon. He wrote—

My brother and I were driving one evening to Chattanooga, Tennessee, from Atlanta. He was driving the car. And for some reason the drivers were very discourteous that night. They didn't dim their lights; hardly any driver that passed by dimmed his lights. And I remember very vividly, my brother A. D. looked over and in a tone of anger said: "I know what I'm going to do. The next car that comes along here and refuses to dim the lights, I'm going to fail to dim mine and pour them on in all of their power." And I looked at him right quick and said: "Oh no, don't do that. There'd be too much light on this highway, and it will end up in mutual destruction for all. Somebody's got to have some sense on this highway."

That is more true today than it was in the 1960s. In a world where half of the people seem always to want the other half dead, somebody's got to have some sense on this highway. In a world where minor insults become lawsuits, traffic accidents escalate into armed conflicts, and a war can be started by any zealot with pipe bomb, somebody's got to have the good sense to defuse conflict rather than fuel it. Somebody must accept injustice in order to ensure a greater good, turn the other cheek, and walk away. Somebody's got to dim the lights on this treacherous road we're traveling.

Dear God, let that somebody be me.

7

CHARITY

"Love your enemies and pray
for those who persecute you. . . ."

Tuesdays are always busy. I was
up at 5:30 a.m., out the door by
6:00, racing to hit the floor by 6:45.
To get anything done at a large corporation, you
have to be working by 7:00 a.m., before the
loafers show up to eat breakfast in their cubicles,
spam you with urban legends, and trap entire
business units inside glass-walled conference
rooms for yet another pointless meeting. On this

Without forgiveness, there's no future.

—DESMOND TUTU

particular Tuesday morning I wasn't carpooling, so I could set out a few minutes early. Traffic on I-69 was no worse than usual, which is to say that it was insane. Someday I hope to find the cash prize that seems to be offered for occupying the ten feet of pavement directly in front of my car. Six yahoos claimed it between 96th Street and 82nd Street. I dodged between a coed putting on mascara behind the wheel of a Geo Metro and a Freightliner hauling eighty thousand pounds of steel to make my exit—just in time to miss the light at the end of the ramp. By 9:05 I'd had four cups of coffee, answered thirty-two e-mails, completed my budget variance report, and issued a written warning to one of my soon-to-be ex-employees. It was a normal day.

That meant also that I was late for a meeting. I was rounding the corner at a medium canter, balancing a coffee cup on top of a nine-inch stack of manila folders, when I heard Helen Adams say, "Oh my God." Something in her voice went beyond the usual I-can't-believe-those-idiots-in-human-resources tone to display something deeper—like horror. I stopped. She said it again, slower, her voice quavering, "Oh my God." I looked at her computer screen, streaming CNN.com during business hours, strictly against company policy. I frowned and tried to ignore the infraction. Then I watched the video. Then I said it too. Then I watched it again. Then my heart

A Different Kind of Crazy
90

stopped beating. Then I watched it again. And then my heart began pounding as we stood in silence, gaping at the computer screen.

It was Tuesday, September 11, 2001.

our Enemies

Most people don't have enemies. I mean most Americans. I mean most middle-class, middle-income, middle-of-the-road white guys. I mean me. I suppose Dickey Bowers was an enemy of sorts when he punched me in the stomach in third grade. But I haven't seen Dickey for thirty years, and I haven't been in a fight since junior high. The people who routinely annoy me at work aren't exactly on my Christmas list, but they're not enemies either. I get along with most people, including my boss, my ex-wife, and my neighbor with the barking dog. I've never hated anybody in my life. But that changed on 9/11.

Most people who look for a context to think about Jesus' well-known command to "love your enemies" look across the dinner table, not the ocean. If you can smile politely while your mother-in-law ruins another Christmas dinner by asking when you're going to get a "real job," you've done what Jesus said. If we can shake hands and walk away after Michigan beats Ohio State—in Columbus—we're square with the gospel. We treat everybody well, even when they're jerks. But nobody can now pretend that's what Jesus was talking about. Not after 9/11. When people ask me what's different about the world since the Trade Center attacks, I don't talk about terrorism or global politics or airport security. I say, "Nine-eleven was the day I discovered hatred." For the first time, I knew what it was both to be despised and to despise others. For the first time, I knew that there was someone whom I truly wished were dead. That was the day I realized that I had authentic, genuine, honest-to-goodness enemies—people who want to kill me and whom I would gladly have tortured with a red-hot poker. It is no longer possible to breeze lightly over scriptures like Psalm 137—

> O Daughter of Babylon, doomed to destruction,
>> happy is he who repays you
>> for what you have done to us—
> he who seizes your infants
>> and dashes them against the rocks.

Now we know what that means because we've said it, or wished it. And it was on 9/11 that I realized I could never comprehend the meaning of these words of Jesus, so often cited by poets and preachers and peacemakers: "Love your enemies and pray for those who persecute you, that you may be sons of your Father in heaven." Until now, that sounded like a nice bit of poetry, like something out of

Shakespeare. It was lovely, really, but so far removed from experience that I felt no obligation whatsoever to apply it to my life.

All of that is different now. Now I have enemies, and I must go about the hard work of figuring out what it means to love them. It's not something I particularly care to do. Perhaps that's the reason I have a hard time believing Jesus really meant that we should.

Defenses for Hatred

Religious people are particularly good at constructing defenses for their behavior. When we bend or even defy the tenets of our religion, we may use that same religion to rationalize our actions. This is how hypocrites in Jesus' day justified allowing their aging parents to live in the first-century equivalent of rat-infested nursing homes—they declared the money they might have used to assist them as *corban*, a gift devoted to God. This is how religious bigots on both sides justified the slaughter of innocent people during the Crusades—they were defending God's holy land. And this is how otherwise gentle people may justify as an act of mercy the use of torture on helpless prisoners—they're trying to gain information that may save countless lives.

Yet few teachings of Jesus Christ are as undeniably clear as is this command to love one's enemies. Jesus said it. He meant it. He wasn't kidding. If we are to be legitimate followers of Jesus Christ, if we wish to use his name as our brand, printing it on our stationery and calling ourselves Christian churches rather than social clubs, then we must learn to deal practically with this teaching. We must love our enemies.

Many of our excuses for ignoring this teaching boil down to fear. We fear appearing weak before our enemies or allowing them to gain the upper hand. We fear the result of forgiving those who have wronged us. Won't they be emboldened? We don't believe that Jesus could have meant this in any literal way because we can't imagine that this policy could have any good outcome. We doubt God, in other words. We don't think grace works. We believe in the power of force. We believe in the courts and the police and the military. We believe that we can secure our future if we control it. We don't think being "soft on crime" by letting evildoers off the hook can possibly produce a better world.

Jesus knew better. He realized that there is greater power in mercy than in vengeance. He understood that grace doesn't merely sound lovely or spiritual—it is the most effective way of dealing with people. When you treat them decently, accept them as brothers and sisters in the human family, allow them to get beyond the sins of their past and move forward, you apply the most powerful of all social policies. When you love your enemies, they become your friends—or at least they cease to be enemies. Jesus did not preclude self-defense, law enforcement, or the protection of society. He simply commanded us to treat all people decently, to love them and even forgive them, not because they deserve it but precisely because they don't.

But hatred feels better, at least for a while. It is invigorating to be driven by outrage, holy indignation, blind justice. It seems empowering to nurse one's wrongs, holding them close to the heart, remembering daily how we've been cheated or hurt. Yet if hatred empowers, it also consumes. The act of hatred only prolongs the agony of injustice. It binds the hater and the hated in a union of misery. It ruins marriages, poisons children, infects communities, and perpetuates conflict. Hatred can be passed from one generation to the next, ensuring that conflict will endure for decades, even centuries. We wonder what kind of world our children will inherit if we forgive zealots and show mercy to terrorists. We might well wonder what kind of world our children will inherit if we do not.

The church is good at bestowing kindness upon those who deserve it. When friends are ill, we pray for them. When somebody dies, we take food to their loved ones. If they're broke, we'll even give them money. We take care of our own. And that, according to Jesus, makes us no better than thieves and murderers. They also look after their friends. The mark of a Christian, the thing that sets us apart from others, the shining achievement that is a beacon of hope to the world, is that we show kindness not only to those who deserve it but also to those who don't. It is that we love the unlovable and forgive the unforgivable. That's impossible, someone will say. And they'll be right. Which is precisely why to do such things reveals the unmistakable hand of God.

Sooner or later this conversation always gets down to cases, and there is where it gets ugly. We hear stories about callous insults, business frauds, and the rape of children. We discuss ways of dealing with everyone from ungrateful siblings to serial killers, from office rivals to sexual predators.

"Am I supposed to let my daughter-in-law insult me in my own house?"

"How can I forgive the man who raped me?"

"Those people killed my son; how do you expect me to feel about that?"

I offer no pat answer for those thorny questions. I say only that being a Christian has very little to do with how you treat those who love you and very much to do with how you treat those who don't.

IT Can Be Done

Is it possible to do this? Is it reasonable to believe that we can truly love those who have harmed us? I offer this witness.

Alberto Neto went to the police for help after his three-year-old daughter was abducted, but they wanted money in order to conduct a search. When Alberto couldn't pay, the police went instead to investigate a traffic accident for a motorist who had given them two dollars. Alberto went on, by himself, looking for the woman who had abducted his child.

This is Mozambique.

Alberto and his wife, Kateko, lived in Xai Xai, where Alberto worked as a bricklayer. The family had little to spare, but when a teenager named Sonia came to their home in need of help, they invited her in. She was hungry and tired and walked with a bit of a limp, and she told a pitiful story about being rejected by her family and forced to flee her home. Alberto and Kateko took pity on her. They couldn't have known that she was a predator who had targeted their home because she had seen Andrea, their daughter, playing outside. The next morning when Alberto and Kateko woke up, Sonia and Andrea were gone.

Sonia was an inept criminal, however, and left some of her belongings behind, including an identification card. Alberto tracked her as far as Maputo, the vast capital, but since there are no street addresses in that city of some two million people, it was impossible to find her. Months went by. Alberto enlisted the help of Christian aid workers and the human rights league. Detectives were hired. A search was mounted. One day while driving slowly through the muddy, trash-strewn streets of a barrio, Alberto called out, "Stop!" He had seen something familiar. He got out of the vehicle and walked down a small street that was wide enough for only two people to walk side by side. When he returned, he announced with excitement, "I have seen her mother! Sonia's mother—she lives down that street!"

The group went to the police, who agreed to help. Three policemen accompanied them back to the barrio, now well after midnight. They parked a block away from the home, and the police crept up to the house. When they entered it, they found Sonia and arrested her. Alberto now stood face to face with the woman who had taken his child.

As the police questioned Sonia, the entire story became clear. She had been promised four hundred dollars to abduct the child; she had been paid eight dollars. She had delivered Andrea to some men; she didn't know their names. What had been done with her? Sex trafficking? Child sacrifice? Slavery? Sonia didn't know. The police continued their questioning for about two hours, finally demanding that she take them to find the child.

Sonia, confused, exhausted, frightened for her life, attempted to guide the police through the dark maze of barrio streets. Sonia struggled to find the home where she'd taken the child. Was it here? No, there. They walked for hours, Alberto's hope and anger conflicting within him. Would his daughter be found alive? Would this woman ever be punished?

"There," Sonia said finally. "That's the house."

The police stormed into the hovel, shouting, rousing tenants and neighbors alike. But there was no child. No evidence. Nothing.

"This is useless," the lead policeman said. "We'll take her back home." Their hope was to find Sonia's mother and "question" her, by which they meant torture. Sonia was little further use to them.

Meanwhile, a crowd had gathered. As they walked through the narrow streets, the word spread—here was a child predator in their midst. Insults were hurled, then threats. There were three policemen, but a crowd of more than fifty people followed them down the narrow alleys. "Let us have her," someone shouted. "Let us question her. We'll get the truth!"

The police quickened the pace. "Keep moving," an officer called. "We're getting out of here." Sonia was limping, her hands cuffed; she was unable to keep pace.

Here was Alberto's opportunity for vengeance. Andrea was gone, there could be no hope of finding his child alive. One word from him might have incited the mob. A quick shove would have placed this helpless woman in their power. What would he do? What would you have done?

Two eyewitnesses to this event reported to me what Alberto did next. He put his arms around this terrified, confused young

woman—the woman who had stolen his child—and he picked
her up and carried her through the filthy streets to safety.

I don't think it is possible to love one's enemies; I know
it is.

Divine Love

About a week after 9/11, somebody decided to help the
nation heal by creating a urinal insert with a picture of Osama
bin Laden on it. One of them showed up where I worked, and
the traffic in the men's room was brisk for several days. We
couldn't do much but feel helpless and hateful, so it felt good
to express the contempt we felt for our enemy. We whizzed
away. But it didn't help, really. We discovered that crude ges-
tures debase not their object but those who make them.
Thankfully, some manager had the mats removed.

Five years or so have passed, and the anger has abated. I
don't hate Osama bin Laden; I don't even know for sure that
he exists. For enemies, I'm back to my ex-wife, Dickey
Bowers, and my neighbor with the barking dog. In other
words, I have no enemies. But I will someday. Evil exists in
the world. There are people who lie for profit, rape for power,
and kill for pleasure. Sooner or later, I will encounter one of
them. I will again know what it is to feel outrage, injustice,
anger. I will have someone to hate. Then I will have the opportunity to decide if I have been playing at being a Christian or

if I am an authentic follower of Jesus Christ. For the truest sign that I am a Christian is not how I behave when things go well but what I do when they don't. Human beings love their friends and hate their enemies. Only a child of God can love them both.

8

SPIRITUALITY

"For where your treasure is, there
your heart will be also."

Julie Dunn is such a pleasant person that it's difficult to be upset with her. She smiles a lot. She dresses well. She's punctual. That's a tremendous asset in her line of work. Julie Dunn is a real estate agent, and she was smiling on the day she told me that my house had appreciated eighteen thousand dollars in the six years I'd owned it. I'd have been smiling too, except that I would owe half that amount,

It is preoccupation with possessions, more than anything else, that prevents us from living freely and nobly.

—HENRY DAVID THOREAU

plus half the remaining equity, to my soon-to-be ex-wife.

"Are you sure?" I asked. The divorce was not acrimonious, but nine grand is nine grand.

Julie smiled again. Wider. "That's what the market survey shows," she said sweetly. She reminded me that a market survey is different from an appraisal. An appraisal is an expert opinion as to the actual value of a property while a market survey shows an average of the recent selling prices of comparable homes in the area. Whatever. I wrote the check. I was then forty-five years old, and that was the first time it occurred to me that having more money might make my life a bit easier. I had lived a sheltered life.

For most of my first forty-five years, I had lived in parsonages. A parsonage is a home provided by a congregation for its pastor. My dad is a minister, so I grew up in parsonages. When I became a pastor myself, I lived in church-owned housing for another thirteen years. I hated it. It's not that there were no advantages. Parsonages are usually conveniently located near the church, often next door. As a kid, that made it easy to sneak into the sanctuary and play hide-and-seek. As an adult, I realized that it's also handy for volunteers who chronically forget their church key or for transients who need a little gas money. Parsonages are generally decorated in a neutral fashion. Odds are good that your black leather sofa will go just as well with the beige walls and tan drapes as did the previous pastor's plaid armchair. The taupe carpet hides stains well, which makes it ideal for growing families. But it's bland. Boring. Uninspired. A stifling way to live.

If I could own my own home, I thought, *I could paint the walls any color I liked. I could replace these hideous drapes. I could remodel the kitchen. And, I would be living every American's dream. I would be building . . . equity!*

I had overlooked the most significant benefit of parsonage life: freedom from liability. In a parsonage, someone other than the occupant is responsible for utilities and maintenance. When it gets hot, you turn on the air conditioner. When it breaks, you call the trustees. But what was that, I reasoned, measured against the freedom, the sheer joy, of home ownership?

This was the frame of mind in which I had purchased my first home, an antique beauty, constructed sometime during Prohibition, or perhaps a little before. I should have realized that the seller was a bit too eager, that the "country charm" was nothing more than a gravel driveway, and that the "possibilities" Julie mentioned were a leaky roof and dilapidated gutters. I might have been wondering how much it would cost to make the house habitable, but I was too enthralled by the American Dream to notice that I was taking possession of the mother of all white elephants. "Where do I sign?" was the only question I brought to closing.

As I perused the closing statement, a second question occurred to me: "What are all these fees?" There were recording fees, courier fees, document fees, agent's fees, and even "convenience" fees. Every county employee and his brother had lined up to take fifty dollars from me. "Gee whiz," said I, "I never knew it cost so much to buy a house." That was the day I'd met Julie Dunn, and it was at that moment that I saw her smile for the very first time.

Over the next six years, I replaced the roof, the furnace, and the electric panel, cut down four trees, and spent enough money on lawn care to maintain a national park. These things all cost money. Therefore, I hadn't been able to replace the taupe carpet or the hideous drapes. Now it was time to sell, and Julie was telling me that this money pit was somehow worth eighteen thousand dollars more than what I'd paid for it. "Let's list it for one thirty-nine," she said pleasantly. That was the beginning, not the end, of my nightmare. Over the next ten, yes, ten months, I got to know Julie well, beginning on the day I signed the listing agreement. "You've really got to get rid of that carpet," she said. "That'll scare off a lot of buyers. And the drapes. . . ." These minor improvements cost a mere two thousand dollars.

Two months later, in spite of Julie's diligent efforts, I had received not one offer; hadn't even had a second showing. Julie smiled again. "Don't panic," she said calmly. "Sometimes it takes awhile to find the right buyer."

"One who can see the possibilities?"

"Exactly."

Another five months went by, and Julie suggested lowering the price. "The market for older homes is really flat right now."

"Flat?"

"Nonexistent."

We lowered the price. After three more months, Julie brought an offer, the first and only one I ever received. She presented it in person. I was beginning to think her smile had been injected.

"Julie, that's less than I paid for the house."

"I know."

"I thought the house was worth more now."

"It was."

"Before I listed?"

"Right."

"But now . . ."

She smiled.

"This house has a brand-new roof. And a furnace."

"All houses have roofs," she said. "That doesn't make them more valuable. And yours has termites."

"Had," I reminded her. "I paid the guy twelve hundred bucks to get rid of them."

"Right. And your basement leaks."

"Only when it rains. What should I do about this offer?"

She smiled. "You can take it or leave it," she said, as if I hadn't known that.

Ten days later we went to closing, again, Julie and I, with the recording fees, and the title insurance, the convenience fee. She brought her smile, and I brought a check for nine thousand dollars. It cost me eighteen thousand dollars to sell my house, not counting the drapes and the termites.

And as I drove home from the closing, nursing the two gallons of gas that would have to last until payday, I turned on the radio. A Christian station was airing one of those call-in shows where people tell all their problems and the host tells them they would be happy and prosperous if only they were better Christians. This show was about household finances, and the caller, a housewife from Dayton, complained that there never seemed to be enough to go around.

"My husband and I fight about money every month," she said plaintively. "We work as hard as we can, but we never seem to have enough."

"Listen to me," the host said emphatically. "I'm going to tell you something that will change your life."

I leaned forward. No one was ever more ready for financial advice than I was at that moment.

"More money is *not* the solution to your problem," the speaker asserted. His co-host clucked agreement. "If you have a financial crisis, more money is *not* the answer."

"That's crap." I said it right out loud. "*Crap!* It just cost me nine thousand dollars to get rid of that shack. I've handed money to roofers and electricians and carpenters and exterminators."

I was raising my voice now. "I've paid to get rid of water damage and mice and termites. I've paid for insurance and depreciation and real estate taxes and commissions." Other motorists were staring at me, sitting in my little car, talking back to the radio. "I've shelled out for every scam from home inspection to radon gas removal, and I can tell you for sure, there's not a problem in the world that can't be solved with *M-O-N-E-Y!*"

I took a breath and stopped for a red light.

It's true, of course. Money can solve nearly any problem and make life nearly anywhere more pleasurable. That's the world we live in.

But we are not of this world. Christians belong to a different kingdom, one that holds different values. And that is nowhere more apparent than in a discussion about money.

THE WRONG CURE

It is often said that Jesus said more about money than about any other subject. I doubt it. The word *money* appears thirty-four times in the Gospels; variations of the word *forgive* appear thirty-nine times. Could anyone read the Sermon on the Mount, for example, or the Gospels themselves, and believe that money was the main thing on Jesus' mind? Or do we fixate on Jesus' financial advice because it, like his teaching on sex, contrasts so starkly with our own practices? Jesus saw money at best as a distraction to real life, an impediment at worst. Most of his followers seem to value money in a much different way.

The easiest resort at this point would be to trot out the same tired statistics that have been cited for decades, showing that North Americans consume a disproportionate percentage of the earth's resources, that we have a lot, waste a lot, and give away comparatively very little. This is one approach to Christian teaching on money: to show that (a) money is evil, and (b) we should feel rotten for having it. The desired result is that we should give money away, generally to the person doing the teaching. The second approach is to show that (a) money is good, and that (b) God wants us to have more of it. The desired result, usually, is that we should pay for additional financial counsel, again from the person doing the teaching.

Jesus' teaching resembles neither of those common ways of thinking. Money was as necessary for Jesus' survival as it is for our own. He did not renounce material things or the need for them. He fasted for forty days in preparation for ministry, then lived on the donations of his followers, often sharing meals in their homes. He ate food. He wore clothes. He slept indoors, at least some of the time. He had a treasurer. That treasurer was Judas, who betrayed Jesus for money, which says more about our use of wealth than about Jesus'. Jesus used money as the necessary tool for conducting his work; Judas saw money as an opportunity to enrich his life. That is the essential difference between Jesus' thinking on the subject and our own. It is not that money is to be either avoided or sought but that the love of money is a shipwreck for souls.

That sad truth is illustrated at least two other times in Jesus' ministry. When a rich young man came to Jesus asking what was necessary for salvation, Jesus told him to obey the commandments. Realizing perhaps that salvation is not a matter of the hands but the heart, the young man pressed Jesus for more. He got more. "Sell everything you have," Jesus told him. "Give your money to the poor, then follow me." The young man couldn't do it. It was not money alone but the love of money—or perhaps the love of the lifestyle that money afforded—that was his undoing.

Later, Jesus entered the Temple and was appalled by the chaotic scene he observed. Vendors were selling small animals to be used as sacrifices. Moneychangers hawked their services to pilgrims. The raucous, chaotic scene closer resembled carnival than the house of God. In this atmosphere, it was impossible to worship. Money—in this case, making money through commerce—had come between God and his people. Jesus turned the tables and sent both vendors and bankers flying. But again, money wasn't the problem, for God himself had prescribed that sacrifices must be made and taxes paid. It was greed that made Jesus angry, the placement of financial gain ahead of worship. You need money, but Jesus taught that you can't love both it and God at the same time.

Jesus met with rich people just as he did with poor people. The prophets warned against showing favoritism to the poor in the legal system—not that that's ever been a consistent problem. Still, the principle exists: rich people are not to be treated with favoritism, and neither are the poor. The problem is not that we have money but that we value it too much and use it in the wrong ways. And, like most people in Jesus' day, we're oblivious to the way it affects our spiritual lives. We use money the way an addict uses crack, blowing through it as fast as we can in search of a better high. We spend it not because we need things, but because shopping is fun. We drive massive vehicles not because we need heavy-duty transportation but because we like to feel powerful. We trade up from one videogame system to another, not because one is obsolete but because the next promises to be more entertaining. At the root of our addiction is the belief that spending money will solve our problems.

It hasn't worked yet.

We make more, spend more, and borrow more than any people who have ever lived, yet we are no less bored and perhaps even more miserable. We attempt to solve problems using money that money simply can't solve—like boredom and guilt and poverty. Spending money doesn't cure our ills, social or personal. At some level, we know that there are things money cannot buy. Still, we keep trying.

A BASIC CHOICE

It is paradoxical that many wealthy people are frugal, while many poor people are spendthrifts. That fact demonstrates that our attitude toward money, not money itself, is at the heart of the problem. As Paul told Timothy, the love of money is at the root of all kinds of evil. We err by placing the wrong value on money, and that value is determined by a prior choice that, once made, will determine the value we place on all things.

There are really two worlds, Jesus said, two kingdoms. One is material. You can see it, touch it, and enjoy it. It's all around you. The gasoline that powers this world is money. The other kingdom is spiritual; it is the kingdom of heaven. You can't see it or touch it, but you can enter it and live as one of its citizens. The fuel that powers this kingdom is love and its sister virtues, grace, truth, mercy, and peace. Love— that is, treating others as you yourself would like to be treated—is the only way to gain self-respect, security, and peace of mind in this kingdom. Money is worthless here. It takes on value only insofar as it advances these higher goals.

So the value we place on money is determined by our prior orientation toward either the kingdom of this world or the kingdom of heaven. Those who see only the first kingdom will be lovers of money. And why not? It powers the only world they know. Followers of Jesus, however, focus their attention on

God and his eternal kingdom. To them, money doesn't matter quite so much. It may be a necessary tool, but it is a nonfactor in most decisions and certainly is not an object of desire.

How do you know which world you're living in? That's easy to tell, according to Jesus. It will be revealed by the things you value most. What matters more to you, homes and cars and clothing and food and toys? Or love, joy, peace, honor, and trust? Do you derive greater satisfaction from things or from relationships? For in the world according to Jesus, there is money on the one hand and God on the other. They are the symbols of opposite worldviews, and you cannot love both at the same time.

A MEANINGFUL LIFE

As I ponder this choice, I'm sitting in a simple, concrete-block home in Monrovia, Liberia, a city of some half a million people that has no water system, no sewer system, very little electricity and even less health care. I'm reading a magazine by the dim glow of a fluorescent light. The forty-five-watt bulb is powered by a gas generator in the backyard. My friends, Larry and Cindy Marshall, run the generator for a couple of hours each night so they can read, flush the toilet, watch a DVD, or otherwise act as if they're back home in South Dakota. I'm here with my wife and son on a one-week visit, learning what it's like to live in a place where the contrast between the two kingdoms is even more stark than at Disney World.

Today we visited Mandetown, a tiny village outside the town of Salala, roughly fifty miles away. To get there, we drove Larry's Toyota Forerunner maybe five miles off the highway on a side road. I've seen better maintained off-road trails in the Rockies. We crossed two fords, one of which was about as deep as the running boards on the Forerunner, and four palm-log bridges with more daylight shining through them than a Florida sunrise. The five-mile trip took just under an hour. We made good time.

Our host for the day was David Mande. He lives in Mandetown, where he pastors a church, chairs the local livestock committee, and oversees the operation of a school that serves one hundred and thirty children. Pastor Mande has five kids of his own, and he takes care of another ten "rice eaters," as he calls them, orphans or local children whose parents are unable to provide for them. When Pastor Mande needs to go to town to buy medicine for his brood or to sell the produce from his small farm, he walks the five miles of bad road. I asked him about that, like the dumb American that I am. "Wouldn't you like to have a bike?" I said.

He smiled patiently. "I would love to have a bicycle," he said. "But for now . . . I will pray to God." Yeah. Pastors who live in mud houses in West Africa tending fifteen children can't easily afford bicycles. Even if he'd had the money,

Pastor Mande would likely have put it toward a metal roof for the school rather than a bike for himself.

So I'm sitting here reading my magazine, a cycling magazine that I brought with me from the States. In a previous issue, the editors had posed this question to their readers: "What's the perfect number of bikes to own?" This issue reported their answers.

"Thirteen," said one reader from Pennsylvania. Another said, "One for every place I spend the night." "You should always be one new bike away from a divorce," opined a reader from California. A cyclist from Connecticut took a page out of J. Paul Getty's book: "Just one more."

I'm not one to talk; there are seven bikes in my garage right now.

And Pastor Mande wants one, just one, not so he won't have to do distance training on his mountain bike or will have a spare bike for the condo. He wants one bicycle so he can ride to the distant farms to check on a community livestock project or get to town quickly when one of his fifteen kids needs an antibiotic.

No, I don't think I need to give away everything I own. I don't believe that for me to have nothing will ensure that anyone else has something. And I can't buy a bicycle for every barefoot preacher in Africa. I don't feel guilty about having a bike—or two. I just wish that I used my bikes for preaching the gospel or buying medicine or something else besides keeping my fat rear end in shape. I wish I had sense enough to use the money God gave me as a vehicle for doing something useful in the world and not just a means of making my own life better. I wish I weren't selfish, shortsighted, and addicted to comfort.

So here's what I'll do: the next time I get bored and feel like having one more thing in my garage will be my ticket to a happy life, I'll go out and buy a bicycle.

And I'll give it to David Mande.

6

TRUST

"Therefore I tell you,
do not worry about your life. . . ."

I f you want to see a preacher get uncomfortable, I mean really itchy, get hold of the microphone during testimony time and don't let go. Most churches don't have testimony time these days, a kind of open mic in the service when people give a shout-out to God. "Who'll stand up and praise the Lord?" preachers used to ask. Then people would pop up all over the congregation

I claim not to have controlled events, but confess plainly that events have controlled me.

—ABRAHAM LINCOLN

and say things like "I'm so glad I'm saved!" or "I just want to bless his name tonight." Then they'd go on about how grand it is to be a Christian. So few of us know why we're Christians these days that it doesn't make sense to have testimony meetings. But we once did that in my tradition, and people gave unrehearsed, if predictable, testimonials about whatever God seemed to be doing in their lives. As churches grew in size, it became hard to hear what people in the congregation were saying, so some churches began using microphones for testimony time, sort of like they do on *Oprah*, not that I watch it. As a younger person, I enjoyed testimony time for two reasons. First because every minute of testimony time was one minute I didn't have to listen to a sermon, and second because you never quite knew what people were going to say.

Such was the case one bright summer day when Danny Angelo, the ne'er-do-well son of Dan Angelo stumbled down the main aisle of our church, just before the close of the service. The assistant pastor had just given a prayer, and Danny motioned as if he'd like to say something to the entire congregation. He was asking to testify. The assistant pastor glanced toward the pastor, seated behind him on the platform. The pastor nodded an affirmation, which was about all he could do. Were we the kind of church that would refuse anyone the opportunity to praise the Lord? Would we give the devil a victory by sticking with our dull, familiar order of worship when the Spirit was moving some soul to bless the name of God?

Apparently not.

Danny, wearing a rumpled overcoat that he might have slept in, his matted hair sticking out at odd angles, tried to mount the platform steps, but the quick-thinking assistant had sense enough to stop him. *Stay there,* he motioned. *I'll hand you a microphone.* What followed was a confused, alcohol-fueled monologue that catalogued each of the young man's sins over the past fifteen years. He allowed that he'd been a drunk and a sinner, but he was trying to get right with God. He slurred his way through his unhappy adolescence, his wayward youth, and into his drug-laced twenties, adding frequent references to the lavish, unmerited grace of God. At one point, I thought he would break into a rendition of Kris Kristofferson's "Why Me, Lord?" The scene went from interesting to humorous to embarrassing, arriving finally at painful, and the face of the pastor registered each passage in a deeper shade of crimson. The helpless pastor had two options. He could (a) sit there like a boob and smile until the drugs wore off and Danny sat down, or (b) go for the microphone and risk having a wrestling match with a drunk in front of four hundred people. He chose option (a), and 399 people looked helplessly on.

One person did not. Dan Angelo got up from his seat on the center aisle, stood erect, turned toward the door, and walked out. The elder man had survived a tour of duty in Korea. He had served as a missionary to the remotest parts of Africa. He had been a soldier, a pilot, and a man of God for over fifty years. He had done, or could do, nearly anything on earth. But he couldn't stop his only son from making a fool of himself in church, and he couldn't sit by and watch it happen.

This is not the kind of thing that should happen in church on a Sunday morning. It is not the kind of thing that should happen at all. And nobody seemed able to do anything about it.

TRUST BEYOND BELIEF

Trust is a word Christians use liberally. It has its root in the idea of faith, and faith is what we're all about. Do we trust God? Of course we do. We believe that he exists. We believe that Jesus is his only Son. We believe that he died on the cross and rose again. We believe, and we are saved.

Yet trust and faith are not the same, or at least they are nuanced differently. To have faith, as we Christians use the term, is to hold something as true. We believe that God exists: we have faith. To trust, on the other hand, is to treat something as reliable, to take action based upon that belief. I can believe that a bridge is sound, but I can't say that I've trusted it until I have walked across. And there's the rub. For in order to trust something, anything—a log bridge, a fifty-dollar bill, God—one must take the chance that it may not be trustworthy. Trust involves risk. Therefore, to trust God is to do more than simply admit he exists. Even demons do that. To be a God follower in the pattern of Jesus Christ, to be a Christian, is to live according to God's way of thinking, which contrasts so sharply with our own. It requires that we surrender control over our lives, putting God and the values of his invisible kingdom first in spite of our counterintuition and believe it will all work out for the best.

That can be challenging for people such as ourselves, who are conditioned to believe that the world works best when it works on our terms. We believe that money insulates us from hardship, so we make acquiring wealth a significant goal. Jesus, on the other hand, said don't worry about where your next meal is coming from; do what's right and trust God to provide. We believe that powerful people have easier, better lives than those who lack power. Jesus said that the first in this life will be last and the last first. Could that be true? We believe that when somebody hits you, the best thing is to hit them back, harder, because survival goes to the fittest. But Jesus said to love your enemies and not to resist evil people. Will we risk that?

Generally, the answer is no. We behave as if we must control our own circumstances in order to survive. We use money as a way of insulating ourselves from pain or failure.

We secure our way of life by building fences and patrolling borders and fighting wars. We control our happiness by controlling our sexuality. Health is our Achilles' heel. In an effort to master it, we annually spend about one-fifth of our gross domestic product, some $140 million, on health care. Some of us die anyway. Like Dan Angelo, we are powerful, capable people. There is nothing we haven't done or can't do. So the most frightening thing God asks from us is not to admit that we're sinners ("Sure, I've made some mistakes") and not to be generous with our income (we've got extra and we know it). The most difficult thing he asks is that we relinquish control of our lives, departing from the rational, sensible, carefully devised plans that we have made and live by a completely different, seemingly irrational, standard.

Here we are, with our wealth and education and preeminence in the world community, living comfortable lives. And there is Jesus, loving his enemies, having compassion on the weak, and giving little thought to where his next meal is coming from. And all he can say by way of explaining this unusual way of life is, "Trust me."

To trust is always to risk. If the bridge fails, I'll fall twenty feet. If the bill is bogus, I'm out fifty bucks. But if God doesn't come through for me, then I've lost everything. And that's a chance most of us are simply unwilling to take. So we sing our praise songs and write our tithe checks and send our kids to good schools. But when it comes to making hard choices between moral purity and sexual satisfaction, honest dealing and financial gain, or social justice and lower prices at the gas station, we choose our own comfort every time. Our money may say "In God We Trust," but the way that we spend it demonstrates quite clearly that we don't.

overcoming fear

I imagine that it was painful for Dan Angelo to walk out of church that Sunday morning. Yet he had to have realized long before that he had no real power over his children. None of us does. We live in a world that we do not control. God does too. While he exercises ultimate authority, he has ceded a portion of it to others. His own creatures routinely defy him and get away with it, at least for now. Like Dan Angelo, God looks on, heartbroken, as his children embarrass themselves.

What the elder Angelo may not have realized is how little control he had even over himself. When he walked out of church that day, did he realize, I wonder, that his own days were numbered? Did it occur to him that in spite of having fought a war, traveled the world, and climbed every mountain in view, he would suffer a stroke and die within a few years? Perhaps not. The illusion of control is hard to shake. We exist at the whim of Providence. Earthquakes, strokes, wars, droughts, cancer, crime: these things happen as they will. The rain falls on the unjust and the just. Nobody knows what tomorrow holds. The secret to living fully, Jesus knew, is not to control your life—you can't anyway—but to live each day as a fully devoted child of God, to love, to work, to laugh, to cry, to bless and be blessed all for the glory of him who made you. It is to put God and his kingdom first, to trust him and let life happen. The secret to a good life is not to control your circumstances but to trust God.

All believers seem to fear this risk at some point. We harbor the secret anxiety that we may come to the end of our lives and discover that we've missed something. We fear not having enough money or pleasure or whatever we see as giving life meaning. Nobody wants to die with regret. Peter spoke for all of us when he brought that up to Jesus one day. When Peter realized the risk he had taken by following Jesus, he said, "But, Lord, we've left everything we have to follow you." I can see the fear on Peter's face. *I gave up everything,* he thought. *Will I die with nothing?* Every disciple faces this moment. It's terrifying.

Jesus understood that. He said to Peter, "Here's the deal: nobody who has sacrificed anything to follow me—home, family, career, whatever—will lose out in the end." You're not wrong, in other words. You're not being stupid by living this way. You always gain more than you lose by trusting God. To follow Jesus, you must abandon the way of life that you have known, and you must believe that Jesus is right to lead you in a different direction. You must trust him. Relax. It's the right thing to do.

LeTTInG GO

I was about sixteen when Danny Angelo disgorged his conscience in front of the whole church. I thought very little about it at the time, but that scene has come back to me over the years, especially as I've discovered how painful it is to see my own children edging out from under my authority. Children provide the surest proof that we do not control the world in which we live. That lesson comes earlier to a divorced parent such as myself. Perhaps the worst part of being a divorced dad is having to put your children on an airplane and watch them slip from your grasp long before you are ready. Like Dan Angelo, you can either sit helplessly and watch their lives unfold or else make yourself absent. Neither option is appealing.

In many ways, of course, divorced parents still have control. We write checks, and there's power in that. We carry suitcases, schedule flights, drive cars. But none of that changes the fact that our children spend much of their time elsewhere. I can choose the airline, and I can reserve the seat, but I can't cancel the flight. I don't have that power over my child's life, or my own.

In truth, I never did. My daughter Lydia is an independent person, an independent thinker. She is destined to be an independent adult. This has always been true. My little fiction is that she will remain, my little girl forever. I kid myself and no one else. While I have been entrusted with her care for a while, I never owned my daughter. And I had no more power to protect her before the divorce than I do now. The rain falls on the unjust and the just. Her fate has always been in God's hands. Now I am learning to let God take care of her when I cannot, something I should have been doing all along.

And when it comes time for my barely teenaged daughter to leave again, I drive to the airport, and I punch the numbers in the little kiosk, and I tell the agent that, yes, my little girl will be flying by herself halfway across the country. I walk her to the gate, and I watch her go through the door and down the ramp. I wait until the monstrous plane lumbers down the runway and disappears into the sky. Then I pray, "Dear God, watch over my little girl. Bless her life, and protect her, and comfort her. Give to her every good and perfect gift that you can think of, and then add one more. Be for her the father that I never was and never can be."

I trust that he will.

10
TOLErance

"Do not judge,
or you too will be judged."

Charlie Trudeau was a good-natured, big-hearted, simple-minded, old man, and everybody liked him. He'd been retired as an auto mechanic for about ten years, but he had a cinderblock garage behind his house, where he still worked on cars for just about everybody. Charlie drove the church bus, and on Wednesday nights he

Years ago I recognized my kinship with all living things, and I made up my mind that I was not one bit better than the meanest on the earth. I said then and I say now, that while there is a lower class, I am in it; while there is a criminal element, I am of it; while there is a soul in prison, I am not free.

—EUGENE V. DEBS

maneuvered that yellow tin can through a maze of trailer parks to haul a load of Ritalin-deprived tweens to kid's club. Charlie couldn't hear too well or he never could have stood the noise. The guy would do a favor for just about anybody, and people respected him, even if he was a dime short.

Some busybody called the city about the mess in Charlie's yard—a pile of wood from a tree he'd been cutting down for about six years. The code enforcement officer cited him for some violation or other, and Charlie envisioned Armageddon. "They'll take my house," he moaned. "Or fine me a thousand dollars." In his mind, that was worse. Some of the guys from church organized a workday and cleaned the place up.

On Sundays Charlie came to church with his girlfriend, Mavis Pratt. They sat toward the back, smiled benignly through the entire service, which neither of them could hear, then went to dinner at the Iron Skillet. They were harmless old people, and I paid them very little attention.

Then one day Donita Ramsey stopped by the church office to gossip with my secretary. After pestering Stephanie for twenty minutes, Donita poked her head through my doorway. "Busy?" she chirped. After gushing implausibly over my last sermon—probably the worst I'd ever preached—Donita ambled around to the real reason for her visit, casually mentioning that Charlie Trudeau and Mavis Pratt were living together, as in cohabitating.

"You're kidding."

"But I'm not supposed to know that," Donita whispered, "so you can't tell anyone I told you. But they *are*, well, you know."

"What?"

"To*gether*."

It is instructive that Adam and Eve were punished for the original sin of possessing too much information. Some forms of knowledge are too terrible, too dangerous, to be rightly held by anyone but God. The knowledge of nuclear fission is like that. So is the knowledge that an eighty-year-old widower and his seventy-four-year-old girlfriend are having sex. Yet having received this information from Donita, I understood that everyone in the church—everyone in the county—had already been told, or would be by the end of the day. I was the last to know.

But I did know.

I knew also that I had to do something about it. As the pastor, I was responsible to ensure the moral purity of my congregation. Sex outside marriage is fornication. Fornication is sin. Sin must be confronted, and sinners disciplined. If I did nothing about Charlie and Mavis, it would be an admission that sex among unmarried people is a matter of no concern. At thirty or so years of age, filled with zeal for the gospel and optimism about the body of Christ, I was determined that everyone in my congregation should know exactly how important sexual morality is and that they should all behave right—teenagers, old people, everybody. Young men are like that, brimming with passion for whatever cause they believe in. I imagine the apostle Paul was about thirty when he ran the coat check at the execution of Stephen.

Yet if I had plenty of ardor, I lacked fortitude. The mantle of spiritual leader felt large on my shoulders, and I wanted moral support. What I needed was backing, a consensus for doing the arduous work of confronting sin. So I decided to pay a visit to George Ellis, a weathered old construction boss who had Solomon's wisdom for dealing with ticklish situations. I explained the matter to George, holy anger rising in my heart with every word. We couldn't tolerate sin in the camp, no sir. Sure, everybody liked Charlie, but that was no cover for evildoing. Let the church be the church! I declared my intention to go see Charlie and tell him to cut it out with Mavis and move back to his little house in town. When I figured I'd whipped George's indignation into a righteous fury, I asked him to come with me.

George said nothing for quite a while, and when he spoke, it was slowly. "I couldn't advise you to do that," he said.

Nervous tension always makes my throat constrict, so my voice cracked a little when I said, "But . . . this is wrong, isn't it? I mean, they're not married."

"It could happen to anybody," George said.

I blinked.

He looked down as if he didn't know what to say, or didn't want to say it. After a minute or two, he said, "Life lasts a long time. Who knows what circumstances any of us might find ourselves in." He looked away. "I'd leave it alone."

"I see," I said in falsetto.

But I didn't see. I didn't see anything of the kind. What I could see was that two people in my congregation were cohabitating in broad daylight. That knowledge burned a hole in my pocket like a twenty-dollar bill. I had to transfer the responsibility for this awful truth onto someone else. Like Charlie. It was in this frame of mind that I went to Charlie's garage, where I found him working on Clifford Everett's Mustang, and I asked him point-blank if he was living with Mavis.

"I dunno," he said. "I suppose that's what you'd call it."

"You mean you're staying there. At night."

"Well . . . yeah." He looked all embarrassed.

Nakedness exposed. Was this was how Adam felt? I persevered, in spite of my rising shame. "But that's wrong, Charlie. You know it is."

"Yeah, I guess," he said. "But her pension, I mean her husband's pension, she'll lose that if we get married. And our Social Security will go way down." He got a little more animated talking about money. "I don't think we could make it if we got married."

At last, a foothold. I said, "Never put money ahead of doing what's right, Charlie. You've got to trust the Lord to take care of you." I believed that then, and I believe it now with all of my heart.

"Yeah, I guess," Charlie mumbled. I stared at him hard and he hung his head like a pup.

I walked out of the garage feeling something I'd rarely felt as a pastor; I felt pride. I was proud of myself for doing the hard work of church discipline. Yes, it had been difficult, but I'd persevered. I'd told the truth. I'd stood for right. I'd shown sinners the error of their ways and pointed them on the track toward heaven. Yet somehow, in spite of that pride, I wondered if I'd done exactly the right thing. I went home to dinner with my wife and children. I read the paper and mowed the lawn. I lay down to sleep that night. But I didn't sleep. I thought about Charlie. And I thought about myself. And I wondered if God felt the least bit pleased with either one of us.

That was the last time I saw Charlie Trudeau. He didn't move out of Mavis Pratt's house, and he never came back to church again.

Mr. Inside

I more or less forgot about Mavis and Charlie after a while. I noticed that they weren't in church, but I had lots of other things on my mind. Between preaching the gospel, drumming up volunteers for the nursery, and refereeing the fights at choir practice, I had plenty to do besides worry about a couple of stubborn old adulterers. On the rare occasions when I did recall that painful interview in the cinderblock garage, I consoled myself with the thought of Jesus chastising the hypocrites. I've always enjoyed that image of Christ. The angry radical. The fiery prophet. I could picture Jesus wearing long hair and reading Sloane Coffin and protesting the war in Vietnam. Jesus was a baby boomer at heart, I was sure of it. He would tell the truth in spite of the consequences. That's what I had done with Charlie, hadn't I?

A failing common among members of my generation, perhaps all generations, is that they fail to notice the moment when they pass from being outsiders in society to being insiders, from rebelling against their fathers to being fathers themselves. Somewhere amid my reading of theology and taking of ordination vows and stepping into the pulpit, I had ceased to be a zealous young student and had become instead a zealous young clergyman. The quantum difference was that rather than merely criticizing power, I now wielded it. Yet if my position had subtly changed, my orientation had not. For I was still looking outward, eager to right the wrongs of others, not considering that I might have faults of my own.

What was true of me has been true of many of us who call ourselves Christians, especially those among us who accept the label *evangelical*. Once a tiny minority, largely ignored by politicians and the press and our more mainstream Christian brothers, we have reached a plurality. Every U.S. president since Jimmy Carter has made the claim that he was born again; it would seem impossible to be elected to that office without courting the evangelical vote. Our books routinely occupy top spots on the nation's best-seller lists. A word from our more prominent leaders will flood Washington with phone calls, giving us veto power over nearly any legislation. We are not an oppressed people; we are brokers of power. And as we do the hard work of confronting homosexuality, denouncing abortion, and defending the gospel-ordained values of the family, I wonder if we realize that we have shifted from being zealous outsiders to being zealous insiders, and if we know the terrible difference.

I recall that the passionate young Jesus wielded his whip against those who held power, and not those who didn't. To the one caught in adultery, he was a liberator and not a judge. And to his own followers, he said, "Don't pick on people, jump on their failures, criticize their faults—unless, of course, you want the same treatment. For in the same way you judge others, you will be judged, and with the measure you use, it will be measured to you."

I sometimes speculate on how Charlie Trudeau might have reacted toward me if our situations had somehow been reversed, if it were I who had been caught in some sexual embarrassment. At the time, it didn't occur to me that I should wonder about things like that. We seldom look for the seeds of sin in our own lives, especially when weeding another's garden.

JUSTICE DELAYED

A month or two went by, and I realized that I hadn't seen Charlie and Mavis in a while. I didn't have to guess why they weren't in church. In a moment of pastoral weakness, I confessed to a friend that I had doubts about my handling of the matter. "Jesus didn't condemn the woman caught in adultery," I pointed out. "It was hypocrites who brought the whole thing up in the first place."

"Ah, but remember the *rest* of the story."

"The rest of the story? He let her go. That was it."

"Yeah, but he told her, 'Go and sin no more.' There's no way Jesus would let that woman off the hook. He *had* to tell her to get her act together. That's the point of the story."

It was a nice twist. My pal had taken a Bible story designed to show God's compassion on weak human beings and his absolute willingness to forgive and had turned it into a morality play. I've done it myself. The first Bible verse I ever learned was John 3:16. Dinosaur that I am, I memorized it in the King James Version of the Bible. During the 1960s it was still about the only version used in churches. "For God so loved the world, that he gave his only begotten Son, that whosoever believeth in him should not perish, but have everlasting life." That verse proves, as any card-carrying evangelical can tell you, that there are only two types of people in the world: those who have made a personal commitment to faith in Jesus Christ and are bound for heaven, and those who are going straight to hell as soon as God turns out the lights. I had memorized that verse before I could write my whole name. It must have been rattling around my brain somewhere when I went to see Charlie about his living situation. *Get yourself saved, Charlie,* was what I wanted to holler at him. *And quit shacking up with Mavis.*

It is odd that I could have drawn a judgmental attitude from the classic verse that describes God's patient, forgiving, sacrificial love for sinful people. It is odder still, confounding even, that we who know or should know the most about God's patience and forgiveness, have developed a not undeserved reputation for being intolerant, unforgiving, even cruel toward those most in need of grace.

Yet we mean well, just as I meant well with Charlie. I was honestly trying to make sense of the whole Bible, including those parts of it that condemn sin—and on occasion condemn sinners. When Paul wrote to the ancient church at Corinth, he addressed people who had become so tolerant of human weakness that they celebrated the immoral behavior among them as a sign of grace. *We don't judge anybody,* they said to themselves.

"What are you, nuts?" Paul wrote. "You've got a guy sleeping with his stepmother, and you're *proud* of it? Throw the bum out!"

We've got to be tough on sin, we believe, because the Bible is tough on sin. We are a city set on a hill; everyone looks to us for an example. If we don't confront those who do wrong, we're just as guilty. It is this thought that underlies the judgmental attitude that so easily creeps into the mind of a Christian and into the discipline of the church, indeed, into the behavior of an entire generation of believers. This is why we favor the death penalty and decry homosexuality and berate legislators for handing condoms to children. We want the world to be right, but it isn't; and we're sure it's our responsibility to do something about it. God hates sin, and we should hate it too. God wants sinners to be punished, and it's our job to warn them. Am I right?

As a younger person, it might have been instructive for me to have read the very next words that appear in the Bible after John 3:16, words that were routinely omitted from my formative religious education. I'd never been asked to read them at Sunday school, let alone memorize them, and they didn't fit well with my in-or-out view of the kingdom of heaven. The words are these: "For God sent not his Son into the world to condemn the world; but that the world through him might be saved." The apostle Peter wrote,

By God's word the heavens existed and the earth was formed . . . By the same word the present heavens and earth are reserved for fire, being kept for the day of judgment and destruction of ungodly men. But do not forget this one thing, dear friends: With the Lord a day is like a thousand years, and a thousand years are like a day. The Lord is not slow in keeping his promise, as some understand slowness. He is patient with you, not wanting anyone to perish, but everyone to come to repentance.

It was never God's desire to punish sinners because it was never God's desire that people should sin. The fact that they did is regrettable even in God's eyes. His greatest desire is not to see them punished but to see them saved. That's true even for reprobates like Charlie. And like me.

Perhaps George Ellis, the lily-livered board member who shied away from chastising sinners, had understood this. I later found out that George, as a much younger man, had been divorced. It happened so long ago that most people didn't even know it, but George's first wife had run out on him. The circumstances didn't matter much in those days. People thought of divorce as only slightly better than blasphemy against the Holy Spirit, so when George remarried he faced a good deal of antagonism, mostly from church folk. George seemed determined to change that single-handedly. Over the years I heard him speak about our little congregation often and say passionately, "Everybody's welcome here. *Everybody*." At first I thought he meant Charlie, and I didn't mind him saying it. Later on I figured he was talking about himself. It took a long time to realize that he was really talking about me.

LIFE IS LONG

"How far you go in life," said George Washington Carver, "depends on your being tender with the young, compassionate with the aged, sympathetic with the striving, and tolerant of the weak and strong. Because someday in life you will have been all of these." As I walked away from Charlie's garage all those years ago, I had no idea how true those words would prove to be. Within a few years, I would find myself back on the outside, like Charlie, feeling the weight of the church pressed against my ugliest, most painful sore. As my own marriage unraveled, finally ending in divorce, I would have my own interview with church authorities, answering unwelcome and embarrassing questions about my personal life.

So this was how Adam felt. This was why he hid. And this was why Charlie had hung his head. And this was perhaps the full meaning of Jesus' words, "With the measure you use, it will be measured to you." The world is round after all.

Once in a while I still think about Charlie and Mavis. They're both up in heaven now, or wherever old fornicators go when they get kicked out of church. I remember them sitting there on the back row, smiling as if they could hear a word of my sermon. And I think about that day in the garage, and the shamed look on Charlie's face, and the fact that neither of them ever came back to the house of God. To this day, I have no idea whether I did the right thing. I am more certain than ever that the holy God demands that his holy people not be found with unlawful carnal knowledge of one another and that those who place their own desires above God's law reap dire consequences. Those of us who know better yet fail to warn others are also guilty, I'm sure of that.

Yet I am less and less persuaded that being a Christian has anything to do with being a cop. If I read my Bible right, Jesus came the first time to forgive people, not punish them. Certainly the Creator of heaven and earth is capable of enforcing his own laws. He can destroy those who oppose him. Yet for the past ten thousand years or so, he has reserved that judgment. Tolerance. Acceptance. Forbearance. Restraint. These words do not describe moral weakness or the love of wrongdoing. They describe God. Therefore, if I am to be godly, that is, to feel as God feels and behave as God behaves, I will love people, grieve for their failures, and be gentle in dealing with their weakness. For when I dispense the potent serum of patience and grace to others, I can hope to receive it myself.

11

FAITH

"Ask and it will
be given to you. . . ."

Friday, December 1, was an
ordinary day in my life. I got up,
went to work, drank about a gallon of coffee,
caught up on e-mail, reviewed a couple of
manuscripts, and went home again. Yadda,
yadda, yadda. That's my life.

Friday, December 1, was also World AIDS Day.
I barely noticed.

Every great dream begins with a dreamer.

—HARRIET TUBMAN

Friday, December 1, also happened to be the day my friend Jo Anne Lyon was invited to the West Wing of the White House, where the president of the United States declared that World Hope International, the faith-based development organization that she founded, had been chosen to lead a 7.7-million-dollar initiative to combat AIDS in the nation of Haiti. POTUS, in effect, handed Jo Anne a check for $7.7 million and said, *Here, go do some good in the world.*

One sec.

Jo Anne is a preacher's kid who grew up in a small town in Oklahoma. I happen to be a preacher's son who grew up in a small town in Michigan. Jo Anne is an ordained minister in a little-known Protestant denomination. I'm an ordained minister in that same church. Jo Anne and her husband, Wayne, pastored a series of churches in the Midwest. I did too. Jo Anne left pastoral ministry to work in a church-related organization. So did I. She's got a bunch of kids. I've got a bunch of kids. She's from the Midwest. I'm from the Midwest. She's a PK; I'm a PK. And she gets up in the morning and goes to meet the president, while I get up in the morning and go sit in my cube.

Other than that, I wonder, what's the difference between her and me?

On the evening of Friday, December 1, I spent a good deal of time pondering that very question. This is what I concluded: Jo Anne believes that God will perform a miracle in front of her very eyes every day, and she acts as if that's true; I believe I'll spill coffee on my shirt, and I nearly always do.

This is the power of faith. It changes the future, for better or worse. And Jesus people, authentic followers of Jesus Christ, are those who believe that God is good and that he's itching to do good things in them and in the world. They are people of faith.

Hard to Believe

We talk a good game when it comes to faith. We use faith words. We *believe* in God. But we generally define our lives, in human terms. We think about living and dying and understanding the world and what it means to be living the good life purely according to what we can see and taste and feel. We talk as if we believe in a personal, supernatural God, but we act as if what you see is what you get. We live as if there either is no God or else he is detached from our lives.

I heard tell of a woman who drove a wedge into that fissure one Sunday morning. Entering a church service already in progress, she ambled down the center aisle, looking around as if searching for someone—or something. Appearing a bit confused, she approached the pulpit and called out to the preacher, "Does it happen here?"

Nobody knew quite what to make of this odd person, so nobody said anything. She asked it again, "Does it happen here?"

Finally the pastor took the bait. "Does what happen here?"

"The sign," she said. "What it says on the sign? Does it really happen here?"

The church sign, posted in front of the building, contained a reference to Matthew 11:5: "The blind receive sight, the lame walk, those who have leprosy are cured, the deaf hear, the dead are raised, and the good news is preached to the poor." The poor woman thought she might see that happen in church on Sunday morning.

No, it didn't happen there, nor does it happen much of anyplace else. I wonder why that is.

Could it be because we doubt that God will be present when we meet, or that he will do anything significant if he should elect to attend? Our worship services are well done, to be sure. They are expertly planned, flawlessly executed, and present an agreeable symmetry. But we never aim for much that we couldn't hit on our own. While we offer an invocation at band rehearsal or drama practice, we don't truly expect that God will show up and cure someone of cancer, reconcile estranged spouses, or change the heart of a lost soul. We get nothing because we ask for nothing. And we ask for nothing because we believe not in God as a person but in God as an idea so remotely connected to our lives that he bears little relevance.

In practical terms, we treat God like the weather. He may offer a bit of sunshine to make our day brighter, or he may annoy us with rain or hail. But his presence or absence makes little difference one way or another. As with the natural elements, we've found a way to work around him. We can have our picnic indoors if it rains. And we can have church and conduct our missions and construct our buildings and be quite content whether God shows up or not.

For the most part, we live our lives outside church in the same manner. We attempt in our work only what is clearly possible on our own. The reason so few of us receive 7.7-million-dollar grants to treat AIDS is that so few of us believe God will provide for our needs in such a spectacular way. When we do feel lucky, we buy lottery tickets. In the lottery the odds are guaranteed, if extremely small; there is at least one winner every week. As for God? Who knows what he'll do, if anything. We have lost faith in the dashing, daring, Red-Sea-parting despot who can do anything and probably will. We no longer believe in a world where anything is possible. We no longer believe in miracles.

Oddly, as children, we never blinked at the notion of the supernatural. We firmly believed that reindeer flew or that animals talked or that angels walked the earth. We greeted these ideas with delight. We saw possibility in them. They helped us to believe that a little boy, with God's help, could kill a giant, or that another kid, with just a few loaves and fish, could see five thousand fed. We practiced saying things like "Speak, Lord, for your servant is listening" just in case we'd ever hear God's voice in the night, fully expecting that we could. No wonder Jesus told us to think like little kids.

But life is cruel. It wrings faith from children as surely as the tide ebbs and the calendar turns. One day we note that Grandma continues to be ill in spite of our fervent prayer. It occurs to us that the pastor is just a person, after all, and that there is nothing magical about the Lord's Supper. We grow. We sin. We suffer. And our faith in a personal, benevolent, life-transforming, devil-destroying, Lazarus-raising God is put up in a box with Santa Claus and Mr. Ed and Peter Rabbit. Heaven is real enough, we hope, but that is for another time. For now, life is what we see, what we know, what we control. Thank God for doctors, we think, and air-conditioning and air travel and agricultural science. Without them, we'd be completely helpless.

The reason you don't have what you need, Jesus said, is because you don't ask for it. And the reason you don't ask for it, he might have added, is because you don't believe that God can provide it, or you don't believe he will. You lack faith.

THE BIG ASK

To believe in God, the God that Jesus believed in, the God he claimed to be, is to believe in a personal, powerful God who is eager to rain blessings on those who seek him. To believe in this God is to believe in a hidden, unseen world where angels and demons wrestle, where a clash of good and evil is constantly taking place. To believe in this God is to believe that he wants ultimately for his will to be accomplished on earth and that he wants for human beings to play a critical role in this grand drama. This is why Jesus came, in part: to demonstrate the connection between heaven and earth. God became a human being. He entered our world. Far from being distant and impersonal, God is human. And he releases his incredible power through human beings.

One day when Jesus was teaching a large crowd of people, his disciples came to him with a problem. The crowd is large, they said, and it's late in the day. You'd better dismiss them so they can go get something to eat. Jesus' response closed the gap between the actual (the kingdom of earth) and the possible (the kingdom of heaven). He said, "You give them something to eat." In other words, you have the power. You feed five thousand people. This may have been the original application of the old cliché, Give a man a fish and he eats for a day; teach him to fish and he eats for a lifetime. Jesus' version? Perform one miracle, and five thousand people eat for a day. Teach them to do miracles, and the whole world will have adequate food.

It was a nice try on Jesus' part, but the disciples looked as blankly at him as if he'd just said, "I'm going to be murdered soon, but don't worry. Three days later I'll rise from the dead." Jesus finally blessed the loaves himself, multiplying food for the hungry. The disciples didn't feed the crowd because they couldn't. The reason they couldn't was not that they lacked power; it was that they believed they lacked power. They couldn't bring themselves to accept the idea that when you trust God, anything is possible.

Jesus believed in a God who is real and close and eager to bless people with good things. He believed God wants the world to resemble his heavenly kingdom, and that transformation will take place when human beings start acting in faith, behaving as if the kingdom has already come and trusting God to close the gap. See a good thing, Jesus taught, ask God for it, and you'll have it. God will make it so, right before your eyes.

Jesus wasn't talking only about doing miracles as we usually think of them. We imagine a miracle being an instantaneous transformation of some ordinary thing. We have one fish, we pray, and, hey, presto, we have five thousand. Certainly that's a miracle. But is it less miraculous to imagine some good thing that doesn't exist—like education in a rural community—to pray, and, hey, presto, generous donors contribute the funds to create a school? Certainly it is a miracle when one person is instantly cured of illness. Is it less miraculous when Christians envision a place where no children suffer blindness, then solicit funding to provide doses of vitamin A to an entire village?

Why aren't there more doctors in Africa? Why do forty million people suffer from HIV/AIDS? Why is the adult illiteracy rate nearly 20 percent in the United States? Why do thirteen million children go to bed hungry every night on the wealthiest continent on earth? It is for the same reason that twelve hapless disciples couldn't figure out how to feed a few hungry people and Matthew 11:5 has been reduced to a motto for church signs. We live with the world the way it is because we do not believe another world is possible. We see no miracles because we do not believe in miracles. We have not because we ask not.

What would the world be like if a few of us—just one or two, or twelve, maybe—began to see the world not as it is but as it could be? What if we began to think of God not as a non-factor in human affairs nor as a mere genie who provides for personal comfort but as a source of power for creating change? What if we believed he was not distant but very close, right here, and eager to release his power through us? What if we began to act on what we say we believe? In other words, what would the world be like if we had faith?

Here's a picture.

Power in My Hand

I was born at the George Washington Hospital in Washington, D.C., on a bright October day in 1959. A day or two later, I was carried into a little church in the D.C. suburb of Franconia, Virginia. My dad was the pastor of this tiny congregation, and I spent the first year of my life there. The next year, my family left Virginia. I never looked back.

Wayne and Jo Anne Lyon did, however. In the summer of 2000, Wayne assumed the pastorate at that same church where my dad had been, the same church where I spent the first year of my life. A lot had changed in forty years. The area was now part of the city of Alexandria and had been enveloped by urban sprawl. The community had also changed colors as immigrants from all over the world migrated to the Washington area. Africans, Koreans, Colombians, Vietnamese, and many other ethnic groups were strongly represented. As Jo Anne was working to take the kingdom to far-flung places like Mozambique and Cambodia, Wayne was faced with the challenge of assimilating the whole world into a single congregation. Many white congregations faced with this situation choose to move farther out in the suburbs or become a sort of enclave within the urban scene. Wayne and his congregation chose to stay and to assimilate themselves into the world culture that had enveloped them. Now called United Wesleyan Church, the congregation has grown from a hundred or so to more than six hundred, with two campuses and worship services held in several languages. I visited my birthplace not long ago, and I lost count of the ethnic groups I encountered—Africans from several countries, Latinos from all over South America, Koreans, Indians, and others.

Six hundred people out of the six billion on earth is not a significant number, really. Yet it is a teeny little glimpse of the whole world, the whole Kingdom, right there in the church where I was born. And it exists because someone had the vision—the faith—to believe that it could be so. The things we dream become reality. This is not hubris or vanity. This is the God-ordained method by which the Kingdom comes. We see justice on earth when there is no justice. We see it because it exists in heaven, and we ask that God's kingdom shall come on earth.

And it does.

As I sat thinking on Friday, December 1, I determined something for myself. I determined that I will no longer dream of making money or buying fast cars or retiring someplace warm. I will not dream of things for myself. And I will no longer look at the long stretch of a day and see only stacks of manuscripts and coffee spills. I will look beyond the office walls, beyond the horizon, beyond this world as it now is. I will see peace. I will see justice. I will see healing. I will see hope for all people. And I will dream that these things, so abundant in heaven, will become real on earth. And I will say to God, "Empower me and I will make it so, right here, right now."

And he will.

12

KINDNESS

"Do to others what you
would have them do to you. . . ."

The schoolyard is not a place where political theory is taught; it is a place where political theory is experienced. It is there, under the inattentive eye of the playground monitor, that children first explore the concepts of leadership, subjugation, rebellion, and anarchy. For good reason did William Golding choose schoolboys as his subjects in *Lord of the Flies*,

Wherever there is a human being, there is an opportunity for kindness.

—SENECA

a fictional study of individual welfare versus the common good. Few human beings are capable of greater cruelty than are eleven-year-old boys. I know this because I used to be one.

My own grade school was a claptrap three-roomed schoolhouse that had been abandoned by the school district some years before. As I entered the fifth grade, riding the crest of the baby boom, the school board members suddenly realized they needed more space for their burgeoning brood. They determined to rehabilitate old District School No. 7 as a one-grade schoolhouse and sent there, out in the boondocks of eastern Michigan, every fifth grader in the county. Our school sat on the edge of a hundred-acre cornfield. The playground held no equipment—no monkey bars or ball diamond—it was just a field where we could play football or tag during recess, or just be ornery, which is mostly what we did.

A porch had been added to the back of the school, which offered just enough room to crawl beneath it and make a sort of a fort. Several of us did so. We used the pilings of the porch as doorposts, and we hauled in some broken cinderblocks. It was dirty, dark, and cramped, an ideal base of operations for our playground shenanigans. But what's the use of having a fort if there's no enemy to keep out of it? Acting on our intrinsic belief that some people are better than others, a bunch of us—namely me, Dougie Fowler, Fred Havner, and Kenny McCloud—decided that it was our fort and that everyone else should keep out. Brian Avery and

Donnie Jensen wanted to be let into the fort in the worst way, but we laughed at them. When they tried to force their way in, we threw dirt at them, and pinecones and rocks. That's what eleven-year-old boys are like.

One day Brian Avery, who was freakishly tall for a fifth grader, maybe five-foot-six, and weighing well over a hundred pounds, got a little pushy about the fort. He started nagging Fred about it, whining about not being allowed in and complaining that it was unfair. Fred was a little guy, but tougher than anybody I knew, probably from being beaten by his old man for so many years. He told Brian to shut up, but Brian kept on. He threw a couple of insults at Fred, said something about the fort, and then called Fred that name that no fifth grader, then or now, will tolerate. He called him a punk. Fred, in spite of the disadvantage of size, went at the bigger boy like a rabid dog after a bunny rabbit, pushing, punching, biting, and finally holding him on the ground, sitting astride him, and pounding him with both fists. The rest of us stood there like Paul at the stoning of Stephen, watching Brian get pummelled into submission and, by our silence, giving a form of consent. The fight ended when the bigger boy started crying and begged for mercy. Fred got off him and started to leave. Brian offered a hand to shake, hoping that would end the conflict once and for all, but Fred spit on him and walked away.

I made a mental note that I should never call Fred Havner a punk, at least not to his face, and that Brian Avery was not the guy to have watching my back on the playground. It occurred to me that I could probably beat the snot out of Brian also, if it ever came to that, and his esteem dropped significantly in my eyes. I felt a bit sorry for him for being humiliated in front of all the guys. But it was pity and not compassion that I felt, meaning that I did nothing about it. I was sort of glad he wasn't in the fort. Besides, he didn't go to our church. Fred and Kenny did.

All of this was run-of-the-mill schoolyard politics and meant very little. We took it for granted that some people were in and others were not. I didn't really care how Brian and Donnie were treated, because the doctrine of fairness applied only to those inside the circle. They knew this just as well as I did. That's why we had to fight.

our Disease

It would be easy to dismiss this childhood bravado as a form of growing pains, or an isolated act of cruelty, or even a generational phenomenon. We baby boomers were mashed into tiny, overcrowded classrooms, which became petri dishes seething with competitive spirit. When I showed up for school in the third grade, there were thirty-six students and only thirty-five chairs in the room. We learned that we had to compete in order to survive. In high school there were twelve spots on the basketball team and more than sixty kids trying out. To earn a place you had to take it from someone else. Boomers are still kind of nasty that way, but we're not unique. Egocentrism is a part of the human spirit. More than fifty million people were killed by twentieth-century wars, most of them started because people of one race saw another as inferior or because somebody had something—land, oil, diamonds—that somebody else wanted. We have seen too many places like Darfur, Cambodia, Sudan, and Kosovo for anyone to pretend that genocide is an aberration or that mega-lomaniacs are some sort of freaks. This is the way the world works: when you want something, you take it from those who are different from or weaker than you, just like on the play-ground.

Yet none of us are likely to place ourselves in the same category as Pol Pot or Idi Amin. Sure, we may occasionally pretend not to see a waiting car and zip into a parking space ahead of it, but we're not monsters. Yet we are capable of more cruelty than we realize. Add stress to the situation—a gasoline shortage, a flight cancellation, a war—and decent people such as ourselves may be seen stealing from our neighbors, elbowing for places in line, or torturing prisoners of war. All of us are capable of behaving badly.

Why do we do this? Why do human beings so predictably resort to cruelty in dealing with one another? Fear is one rea-son. We fear what will happen if the other kids ever get into the fort. Maybe Brian and Donnie will take over. Maybe they'll kick us out. We treat others badly in order to secure our own position in the world.

Mostly, though, we seem to be guided by the notion that some people are simply better than others. When God handed out nearly everything, he gave a bit more to some than to others: looks, brains, personality, strength. Those who have it, whatever it is, always fare better than those who have not. This is why attractive women get waited on faster in stores. It's why we kowtow to powerful people, even when they're miserly or mean. It's why we give honors, even at church, to people who have done nothing more meaningful with their lives than get rich. And it's why people who are overweight or ugly or have the wrong skin color are often ignored, avoided, or mistreated. It is why churches routinely spend nearly all of their money on buildings, programs, and services aimed at satisfying the desires of those who are already there rather than spending time and money taking the good news to hookers, gangsters, and drug addicts, as Jesus did. For while we may sing "Jesus loves the little children, all the children of the world," deep down we believe that our kids matter more than anybody else's, and we're quite content to close the door of the ark from the inside, secure in our conviction that some people deserve to go to hell—but not us.

seeing others

Fighting on the playground of District School No. 7 made very little impact on me. For one thing, I was smart enough to stay out of most fights, realizing that I would probably wind up like Brian Avery—crying, humiliated, on the outside looking in. I learned instead the art of politics, diplomacy, alliance making. I learned to stay on the right side of the right people. I became best friends with Fred Havner. I don't recall any other lesson from the fifth grade, but I do remember learning this: in order to survive, you must be on the right side of the power equation. You must either have power or have friends who do.

Brenda Flood had neither. Brenda was friends with nobody because she was overweight. When the girls got together on the playground, gossiping or giggling or doing their hair or whatever, Brenda was treated to a circle of backs. To the boys, Brenda was a nonperson. When we took any notice of her at all, we called her names behind her back. Oddly, Brenda seemed oblivious to this. It didn't occur to her that she was the object of cruelty just as it didn't occur to us that we were being cruel. We thought somehow that she must have enjoyed playing the goat.

One day, however, Brenda broke a cardinal rule of the jungle, or playground in this case. She forgot her place. That was easily done, since she didn't have one. As the girls were engaged in a heated discussion on the meaning of "Hey Jude" and the boys were busy stomping on a colony of ants, Brenda wandered off unnoticed and invaded the fort. When we boys arrived there a few minutes later, there was Brenda, under the porch, smiling as if she'd just been handed a fifty-dollar bill.

"What are you doing here?" Fred demanded.

Brenda seemed not to know how much trouble she was in. "Let's play tag," she said, and swatted Fred on the shoulder. "You're it."

"Shut up, you fat pig," somebody hollered. Others joined in.

"Oink, oink. You smell something?"

There were more taunts. All of a sudden, it dawned on Brenda what was happening. "Shut up!" she screamed. "Shut up! You're the pigs." There were tears in her eyes, but she didn't break down crying. She didn't dare show that much weakness. "Shut up!" she screamed again. She knew it. In that moment there, in the dim light beneath the porch, squatting in the dirt, she finally saw the schoolyard as it was. She knew that she was unloved. She knew that she was left out. And she screamed again, "Shut up!"

I saw it too. I saw the whole, awful scene for what it was. I saw the school, I saw Fred, I saw myself. And I saw Brenda. I saw that she was real, like me. I saw that she was afraid, as I had been afraid when I watched Fred bloody the nose of Brian Avery. And I saw that I was on the wrong side of the power equation, the side of fear and meanness and cruelty. I saw it all, but I felt powerless to do anything about it.

"Get out, you pig!" Matt shouted, and pushed Brenda backward. Girl or not, she was about to get the same treatment as Brian or anybody who forgets his place in the world. The thought entered my head that I should help her. I should stick up for her. I should at least say something. I knew this. But I did nothing. I would watch the beating, just as I had watched before.

Then somebody spoke, loudly and with authority. "Shut up, Matt." It was Fred. "Leave her alone," he said, and he pushed in between Matt and Brenda. "She's just a girl." Matt was too shocked to answer back, and no one else dared to challenge Fred. The silence was like that surrounding the woman caught in adultery after Jesus faced down her accusers. Brenda scampered away, into the sunshine, wiping tears from her eyes. She disappeared around the corner.

Things were a little different on the playground after that, but not a lot different. Brenda still kept mostly to herself, and she was less happy now that she saw the world as it truly is. But one or two people talked to her sometimes. I did. Sydney Ellen Johnson did. And Julie Cantrell sat beside her at lunch now and then. Fred never spoke to Brenda, as far as I could tell, but I had a feeling that he had seen the same thing I had seen under the porch. I think he saw that being on the winning side and being on the right side are not necessarily the same thing, and that Brenda, like all overweight people, and skinny people, and rich people, and sick people, and black people, and white people, and all people—are people. This is the essence of Jesus' teaching, in playground terms. Everybody else is just as important as you are. They're not threats or objects or jokes; they're people. Rather than treating them as they appear or even as they deserve, treat them with kindness, with fairness—the way you'd like to be treated.

In a world that is almost constantly at war, divided by class, race, religion, and politics, this Golden Rule is difficult to apply. But Jesus never told us to arbitrate age-old disputes, make bitter enemies into friends, or unite the Gordian knot of global politics. He told us to commit the simple act of loving our neighbor. Certainly, world change was an object of Christ's mission. Yet he pursued that goal by creating change in the heart of the individual, a change that would issue forth a ripple of love, tolerance, kindness, and gentleness from one, to two, to four, to sixteen, and finally to the world. When we behave badly in grand ways, we have first behaved badly in smaller ways. We have wars between groups of people because we first have lesser disputes between neighbors. We lack humanity in the end because we lack good manners in the beginning. Jesus didn't say "Don't commit genocide"; but he did say, "Treat others as you'd like to be treated." Kindness is a virtue best shown toward one person at a time.

Had Jesus cared to expound on that a bit, he might have added to that principle some practical behaviors, such as these:

- Invite others to be served ahead of you, especially your elders.
- Greet everyone you meet with a smile.
- Compliment others frequently.
- Don't be critical of someone who tried his best, even if he failed.
- Don't repeat unflattering things about another person, even if they're true.
- Don't tailgate.
- Be on time.
- Lend a hand to someone engaged in a difficult task.
- When entering a building, hold the door for the next person.
- Don't talk with food in your mouth.
- Turn off the ringer on your cell phone when you enter a restaurant.
- Smile frequently.
- Say thank you to those who have served you, even if it's their job.
- Discipline your own children diligently and other people's children not at all.
- Stand when others enter a room.
- Speak pleasantly to waitresses and store clerks, even when they make mistakes.
- Don't insist on having your own way.
- Encourage people before correcting them.

- Don't offer your opinion unless asked.
- Speak well of your spouse, children, and parents in front of others.
- Say little about your own achievements.
- Don't whine when you don't get your way.
- Apologize sincerely when you are wrong.
- When you approach a parking space at the same time as someone else, let the other driver go first.
- Don't talk too much.
- Be tolerant of other people and their shortcomings.
- Treat other people as if they were important, because they are to God.

I wonder what the world would be like if more people behaved this way. I wonder what my school would have been like and how different I would be now if I had learned earlier to treat other people with the same respect that I would want for myself. This is the basis of our religion. This is the basis of our godliness, our holiness. This is the most basic thing that Jesus taught us: we must treat all people with respect, courtesy, and dignity. How, then, can we say that we love Jesus if we do not first love our neighbor as ourselves?

OPEN THE FORT

I don't know what ever became of Brenda Flood. My family moved away at the end of that school year, and I lost touch with all my schoolyard chums. I did hear that Fred Havner and Brian Avery eventually became friends. Several years later, Brian began attending the same church as Fred, the one I had gone to. Fred finally decided to let him into the fort, and I think Brenda's invasion was part of the reason. This is what happens when you begin to see that other people are not so different from you. You make their lives better, perhaps, but you gain as well. The fort becomes a bigger place when you let others in, not a smaller one.

I would like to say that following my fifth grade year, I never got into a fight or insulted a classmate or was cruel. I know that I was. This is a hard lesson to learn, that other people are as important as you are. Maybe that's why Jesus said it so many times in so many ways: the first will be last and the last first; suffer the little children to come to me; love your neighbor as yourself. When we do these things, we become both more human and more divine. We become like Christ.

13

INTEGRITY

"Not everyone who says to me, 'Lord, Lord,'
will enter the kingdom of heaven. . . ."

ll pastors are eager to make converts, and that goes double for young ones, as I once was, who are impatient to make their mark on the church and the world. Yet as the pastor of a small congregation in a rural village, I found few prospects for evangelism. Those I did encounter were pursued with evangelical zeal. One such potential disciple was Jason, a fortyish

At a certain point, I just felt, you know, God is not looking for alms, God is looking for action.

—Bono

man who made his living as a real-estate appraiser. Jason's wife, Leslie, attended our church every Sunday, sang in the choir, and taught Sunday school on occasion. Their fifteen-year-old daughter attended too, whenever Leslie could drag her out of bed. Leslie was forty herself and had begun to experience the fear, common to wives and mothers at midlife, that her looks were vanishing, that her children no longer needed her, and that her husband might not be helpless to her will after all. These concerns had perhaps aggravated her asthma, which had worsened a bit in the preceding year. For a number of reasons, including concern for his eternal soul, Leslie was desperate that her husband should become a Christian. We had something in common.

Jason, for his part, was a decent fellow. He made a good income, was faithful to his wife, and seemed to tread lightly in the world around him. If Jason had a fault it was that he enjoyed the finer things in life perhaps a bit too much and tended, therefore, to be a bit of a snob. If Jason had a hang-up it was that as a Vietnam veteran, he had seen too much of life too soon and was, therefore, a bit of a skeptic. Among his virtues, Jason was a conversationalist and a willing host. He thought carefully about many subjects, including his own life. I saw him as the perfect mark for evangelism: a thoughtful man, interested in discussion, eager to apply reason to his system of belief. I lost no time in engaging Jason in conversations about life and faith. For one or two of our casual meetings, I listened as he talked about his work, the war, his family, and his home. It was perhaps our third encounter when I turned the conversation to religion. I asked Jason, "What do you think of Jesus?" His answer gave me reason to hope.

"I've thought a lot about Jesus," Jason began. "I've read the New Testament, and I think Jesus was extraordinary."

Surely this was a good sign.

"Tell me more about that," I said, recalling the line verbatim from one of my textbooks in pastoral counseling.

"Well, his teaching was incredible," Jason said. "The Sermon on the Mount in particular." I was getting goose bumps. Surely this was a soul I could save. "There's never been anyone like that. Never. And I don't think there will be again. Jesus Christ was. . . ."

"The Son of God?" I offered.

Jason looked at me as if I'd said *vegetable soup* or *Elvis*. "No," he said dryly. "I was going to say 'unique.'"

"Oh," I said. Surely the cause wasn't lost, though. I rallied my wits for another sortie. "So," I asked nonchalantly, "would you say that you are a believer in Jesus?"

"Of course," Jason said. "I mean in the things Jesus taught— to love your enemies, to treat people as you'd like to be treated, to tell the truth and not be a hypocrite—this is just what the world needs. I really think Jesus' teaching is the only hope."

"You mean you're a Christian?" Was my work already done? This was like shooting fish in a barrel. But Jason's next words deflated my hopes.

"No," he said. "I'm not a Christian because I don't believe that Jesus is God's Son or anything like that. He was just a guy. But he had a lot to say, and I've tried to learn from him."

I felt as if I'd been turned down for a prom date. And like a disappointed suitor, I had no better sense than to ask the question again. "Well . . . is there anything that might change your mind?"

Jason hesitated for just a second. He tilted his head, shrugged slightly, and then said without emotion, "No, not really. I've thought about this a lot. I'm not a Christian, and I'm not going to be."

I could hear Leslie wheezing in the other room. I mumbled something like "Thanks for your honesty," as if he'd done a favor by telling me that my belief system was crap. Then I went back to my office and sat in my chair and thought for a long time about how a bright, considerate, clean-living guy like Jason could have all the information I have about Christ and make the informed, rational, passionless choice to walk away.

What did that say about Jesus? I wondered. What did it say about me?

BAD EVANGELISM

People become Christians for all sorts of reasons. And as I discovered in reflecting on my conversation with Jason, people have an equally wide variety of reasons for making converts. I realized that although I had some concern for Jason's salvation, my primary motivation was something quite different. I wanted to do the right thing as a pastor, I wanted the church to grow, I wanted to succeed. If Jason would come to Jesus, I would somehow be a better Christian for having made the referral. I took Jason's denial of the divinity of Christ personally. I felt rejected. If he, an enviable person in many ways, could think different from me on something as crucial to life as religion, then could it be possible that I was . . . wrong? I wasn't looking to save Jason's soul so much as my own. I wanted him to affirm Jesus and by so doing to affirm me. I wanted him to say, in effect, "You're right, Larry. You've been right all along. Thank you for telling me how wonderful all you Christians really are."

I would feel more pathetic about that if I didn't have so much company. The church entering the late twentieth century was as desperate to make converts as I had been, and for the same reason. Our numbers had dwindled, and Western culture had moved away from us. Presidents no longer consulted us. Newspapers no longer printed our sermons. People had quit coming to church. And we wanted to avoid being marginalized—we wanted to survive. We wanted to hear from a culture that seemed more and more affluent, reasonable, and prosperous, "Well done, good and faithful servant. You Christians are all right after all." So we abandoned the idea of presenting to the world the person and claims of Jesus

Christ and presented ourselves instead. Rather than trying to demonstrate how righteous, holy, and forgiving God is, we attempted to show the world how reasonable, decent, and likeable we are.

It worked.

Our churches are now lovely community centers, equipped with the latest sports equipment and childcare facilities. We promote clean living. We're known as good people, morally conservative, fiscally responsible, and law abiding. While it's true that lots of our younger people leave the church in favor of something that seems more real or challenging, every year our ranks grow by attracting people who want not so much to be like Jesus—perfectly Godlike and utterly selfless—as to be like us—prosperous, fit, and upwardly mobile. And that feels pretty darn good.

A question worth asking, however, is what any of this has to do with Christianity; in short, what it has to do with Jesus. Jesus castigated the Pharisees for making converts to themselves rather than to God. He said, "You travel the whole world to make a single convert, and when he becomes one, you make him twice as much a son of hell as you are." What would be Jesus' assessment of our version of evangelism? We convert people, it's true, but from what to what? The number of people who identify themselves as born again has steadily increased over the past couple of decades, yet these same folk live essentially the same lives as their "unsaved" neighbors. Christians are just as likely to divorce, cohabitate, lust, have abortions, or lie to their bosses. What would be Jesus' assessment of our evangelistic practices, which have brought thousands of people to make a profession of faith but relatively few to prize sexual fidelity, renounce materialism, work for peace, or otherwise apply the teachings of Jesus to their lives? Our converts are baptized. They attend church, they vote, they tithe. But their lives are not changed. Is that enough?

WHAT a CHRISTIAN IS

What does it mean to be a Christian? That's the question I pondered after talking with Jason. Jason behaved as most Christians do; better, actually. He believed that the last shall be first, that peacemakers are blessed, and that God is more important than money. He just wouldn't admit that Jesus is the Son of God. I, on the other hand, had made vehement affirmations of every orthodox creed, signed and dated them actually, and would rather have died than renounce the title *Christian*. Yet I recall in those days being sometimes envious, spiteful, materialistic, and self-serving. In spite of my stated belief about the person of Christ, I did not always behave as if Jesus had authority in my life. Was Jason a Christian? Was I?

Over the centuries those who have taken the name of Christ have conceived of that identity in various ways.

Catholics and their fellow travelers have pointed to the sacraments, particularly baptism, as the mark of a Christian. If you're baptized, you're a Christian. Period. If you sin a lot and don't attend mass, then you're not a very good Christian, but you are one. Christianity has been to millions of people a kind of birthright. Like ethnic origin or gender or height, it is something that you simply are. It's a tribal approach to Christianity.

The Reformers and their offspring in the mainline denominations have taken a different view, defining the Christian faith as something you believe. The Christian faith, they would say, is embodied in Scripture and in the creeds. If you agree with all that, then you're a Christian. Christianity is a matter of what you think, what you agree to, what you intellectually affirm. It's an enlightened view of faith. It makes Christianity a matter of doctrine.

Evangelicals have taken yet a third view, defining Christianity as an experience—it is something that happens to you. When you "make a decision" for Jesus, you are "born again." You become a Christian. It's a bit mystical. This was the result I had so hoped to realize with Jason.

Each of these ways of identifying the faith is helpful, and each has a good deal of scriptural support. They're not wrong by any means. But are they complete? Do they apply the teaching of Jesus himself to the question "What is a Christian?"

In one of the clearest statements on salvation ever given, Jesus made this brutally direct warning: "Not everyone who says to me, 'Lord, Lord,' will enter the kingdom of heaven, but only he who does the will of my Father who is in heaven." It's not what you say, according to Jesus, but what you do that is the true indication of your affinity with him. He later said, "By this all men will know that you are my disciples, if you love one another." It'll be easy to identify my followers, Jesus said: look at the way they act. Among Jesus' last words on earth were these: "Therefore go and make disciples of all nations, baptizing them in the name of the Father and of the Son and of the Holy Spirit, and teaching them to obey everything I have commanded you."

We spend a good deal of time on the first part of this imperative—baptism, or bringing people to the point of accepting the identity *Christian*. We spend far less time on the second half, which is teaching them what Jesus said we ought to do and calling upon them to do it. It is worth noting that Jesus didn't give advice, suggestions, or even mere teachings. He gave commands, and he expected that they would be obeyed by those pledging allegiance to him. When we ignore behavior and conclude that a Christian is somebody who has been sprinkled with water or affirmed a series of propositions or whose name appears on the membership roll of a church or who simply says "I am a Christian" meaning "and not a Jew, Muslim, Hindu, or Buddhist" we ignore Jesus' pointed instruction on the matter. What is a Christian, according to Jesus? It's somebody who does the will of God, someone who behaves as Jesus did.

Over the centuries, Christians have cleverly, creatively, and incessantly ignored the connection between faith and behavior. It would be easier, certainly, if being a Christian were merely an intellectual choice or were some inner, spiritual experience and had nothing to do with everyday life. But it isn't. Being like Jesus has more to do with how we treat other people and handle money than with anything we say or do on Sunday morning.

Jesus didn't come to create a legion of people who had correct beliefs or who were willing merely to worship him (wasn't that the final temptation, which he rejected?). He came to create a kingdom of people who were changed—born again—so that they would think and act different from the world around them. And while it is true that focusing on behavior at the expense of belief produces the bizarre religion of legalism, it is also true that elevating belief at the expense of behavior produces the tepid religion called nominalism. Jesus renounced both, and James added this castigation of the latter: "Faith by itself, if it is not accompanied by action, is dead. . . . You see that a person is justified by what he does and not by faith alone."

What on earth difference could it make to God whether I pay my income taxes? What possible connection could there be between being a Christian and being helpful to my neighbors or environmentally responsible or generous with my friends or unselfish around my kids? What does my religion have to do with the way I drive during rush hour or behave at a ballgame?

Everything.

It isn't the people who talk Christian who get into heaven, according to Jesus. It's the people who act Christian. I'd like to be one of them.

no more questions

Jason was a dilemma to me, and perhaps that was the problem. I tried to solve him like a puzzle rather than know him as a person. I had a prayer in mind that I wanted him to recite. I wanted to show him the bridge illustration, take him for a stroll down the Romans road, then ask him to bow his head and repeat after me. But Jason wasn't interested in formulas and charts. He was too busy living his life. Perhaps if I'd spent less time trying to get Jason to get with the program and more time in true dialogue, I would have found a way to help him step fully into the Kingdom.

Jason still puzzles me. For I am convinced that my experience matters. I came to Christ one day, and he changed me. I was born again. That passage set the course of my life for eternity. Evangelicals aren't wrong about that. Christianity is an experience.

And I'm convinced that my identity matters. Being baptized, being one of the tribe, belonging to Christ and his people, this is who I am, and it pervades every thought that I think and each word that I say. The Catholics aren't wrong about that: Christianity is a state of being.

And I'm convinced that my beliefs matter too. They underlie my daily thoughts and, therefore, my emotions and actions. The Reformers weren't wrong about that: I confess Christ, and I am saved.

Yet I am most of all convinced that my connection with Christ is my life—my whole life, not just my mind or my emotions or my birth certificate. And I often think of Jason, who was not in the Kingdom but who acted as if he were, and I think also of another decent man, a teacher, who asked Jesus what was the greatest of all commandments—the main thing God wants from people—and Jesus told him: "The most important one is this: 'Hear, O Israel, the Lord our God, the Lord is one. Love the Lord your God with all your heart and with all your soul and with all your mind and with all your strength. The second is this: 'Love your neighbor as yourself.'"

The fellow liked Jesus' answer and, not realizing who it was that he addressed, gave Jesus this little pat on the head: "Well said, teacher. You are right in saying that God is one and there is no other but him. To love him with all your heart, with all your understanding and with all your strength, and to love your neighbor as yourself is more important than all burnt offerings and sacrifices."

Here's a guy who gets it, Jesus thought. And he said, "You are not far from the kingdom of God." After that, nobody dared to ask Jesus any more questions.

And when I think about Jason and I think about this good man who was so far from being a Christian but so close to the Kingdom, I usually quit wondering who are the true Christians and who aren't, and I go back to doing the things that Jesus said to do.

14
commitment

"He taught as one
who had authority. . . ."

Mrs. Mitchell was a pleasant old lady, but like a lot of pleasant old ladies, she was a perfect pain in the backside. Not that it mattered much to my dad, who was her pastor back in 1963. Once a week or so, Dad would trudge up the steps to Sister Mitchell's apartment to pay a pastoral visit. In those days, people in our movement called each other "brother" and "sister" to emphasize the egalitarian nature of the church. That was before we started using fancy titles like "reverend" and "doctor" and "reverend doctor." We were a common people and we knew it.

On one of these pastoral calls, Dad arrived just after Sister Mitchell had been reading Acts 4, which says, "All the believers were one in heart and mind. No one claimed that any of his possessions was his own, but they shared everything they had." Inspired by that vision of common concern, she did something quite remarkable, especially in 1963. She gave away her television set.

"Brother Wilson," she began, "the Lord has laid something on my heart. I've got this television set, and I'm here all by myself. I don't need the thing. You have those children at home. You need it more than I do. I want you to take it."

This presented a quandary to my father, who was torn between his pastoral concern and desire for gain. Television sets were something of a rarity in the early '60s. Ours was certainly not the only house on the block that didn't have one. And this elderly woman was by no means wealthy. Living alone in that upstairs apartment, this was perhaps her most significant possession.

"Oh, no, Sister," he said. "I can't take your television from you."

But the old lady insisted. "Yes, Brother Wilson, I want you to have it. I couldn't sleep tonight knowing that I've got this television set all to myself. You must take it."

So he did.

Back in the Golden Age of television, the term *portable* was applied to any TV that could be moved by fewer than two people. Dad lugged this television, weighing about fifty pounds, down the steps from Sister Mitchell's apartment, into the car, and home to our house. My sister and I were thrilled. It was like Christmas morning in July, watching cartoons on that grainy, black-and-white, fourteen-inch screen. We were in heaven.

About a week later, Dad went back to see Mrs. Mitchell, and he found the dear woman in low spirits. Moody, depressed, ill perhaps, it seemed that she wouldn't be long for this world.

"Sister Mitchell," Dad inquired, "are you all right?"

"Oh, Brother Wilson, I shouldn't complain. The Lord is so good to me. It's just that I miss that old television set of mine."

Of yours? Dad thought. *Hmm.* "Well, the kids sure do enjoy that television that you *gave* me," he said. "You should see their faces. I'm not sure how we lived without it."

"I know, Brother Wilson. It's just that I get so lonely here, being by myself all day, with no one to talk to. And nothing to do. That television was my only companion."

She heaved a great sigh.

"I don't suppose you could bear to bring it back to me."

Dad said nothing.

"It's just that I'm so lonely and all. I hate to ask you, but I really do want *my* television set back."

What my dad might have said was some version of the salesman's mantra: A deal's a deal. But preachers aren't allowed to be practical in matters of business. Instead he said, "That's okay, Sister. I'll bring it back to you right away." Later that afternoon, with one child clinging to each of his legs, Dad lugged the old TV out of our house, into the car, and back up the stairs to Sister Mitchell's apartment. My sister and I went back to reading books and playing outside for after-school recreation.

I think Dad skipped a couple of weeks in visiting Mrs. Mitchell after that, and you couldn't blame him. But after a while, he trudged back up the steps to the old woman's apartment for a pastoral call. There, once again, sat a dejected Sister Mitchell.

"Brother Wilson, I've done a terrible thing," she lamented. "I've committed a great sin against the Lord."

Heavens, what could it be?

"It's that television set," she continued. "I've grieved the Holy Spirit, I know I have." Recalling the fate of Ananias and Sapphira, the dear woman was eager to right her wrong before it was too late. She said, "I insist that you take that television set back. It's rightfully yours, and I want you to have it."

"Are you sure?" Dad asked. She was sure. Once again, Dad carted the monstrous thing down the stairs, into the car, and back home. My sister and I did cartwheels across the living room. That is until the next week, when Dad visited Sister Mitchell yet again. And yet again, she lamented the loss of *her* television. And yet again Dad lugged the gigantic appliance out the door and up the stairs to the old woman's abode.

While it may be the case that some writers, especially those who are also preachers, occasionally take a bit of dramatic license in order to make a point, I affirm that what follows is entirely factual. The very next time Dad visited Sister Mitchell, she tried to give him the television set for the third time. That's when Dad finally quit acting like a pastor.

"No," he said firmly. "I won't take it. And what's more, you don't want me to. You're only offering it now because you feel guilty, but in your heart, you know you want it, and you're going to have it. I don't care if you can sleep tonight or not."

Then he left.

And that's what Jesus will eventually do to those who keep declaring their allegiance to him and taking it back, as if he were a parish priest or used car salesman or a six-year-old child instead of what he is—the Christ, the anointed one of God.

YES, BUT

To be fair about it, I don't suppose anybody fully knows what it means to be a Christian when he signs on. We crave forgiveness or we see the beauty of Christ's life, and we want that for ourselves. Rightly so. But we can't know what it means to drink the cup that he drank—to offer our lives fully to God, without reservation—any more than a kid standing in a Marine recruiter's office can understand war. We revel in forgiveness and freedom, enjoying the knowledge that Jesus is our "friend." We change perhaps, in subtle ways. We're not so cantankerous, we drink less, we give some money to the church. But at some point we realize that Jesus is not exactly who we thought he was, and we commence to wonder who he really is and precisely where he intends to lead us.

That moment of realization occurred in the life of Peter on the day Jesus asked his disciples about his reputation. "Who do people say I am?" Jesus wanted to know. After a minute, he narrowed that question. "Who do you say I am?" Peter got it right on the first try: "You are the Christ," he said, meaning God's anointed one. He understood that Jesus had authority in the world. But moments later when Jesus described his impending capture, crucifixion, and death, Peter was appalled. This wasn't the Jesus he'd signed up for. *What have I gotten myself into?* Peter must have thought.

This moment of truth came for the other disciples one night in a leaky boat. They were crossing the Sea of Galilee when a storm arose and threatened to sink their little ship. Jesus lay calmly asleep in the bow. "Wake up!" they hollered to him. "Don't you care if we drown?" It is somewhat troubling to note that Jesus ignored that question. Instead, he rose and loudly declared, "Silence!" then went back to sleep. The storm vanished, and the disciples went white with fear. "Who *is* this?" they asked themselves. Apparently, Jesus was something more than the Bohemian buddy they'd been palling around with. He was the Son of God, perhaps, or the Prince of Darkness. Who knew?

It comes to each of us sometimes, that what-did-I-sign-up-for feeling that whittled Jesus' following from a massive crowd down to a band of twelve and finally to a few women standing before the cross. Every follower of Jesus Christ seems to face this realization that being a disciple demands more than he had imagined. We must then decide either to keep going on this uncertain road or turn back. We must give Jesus our full allegiance or none at all.

Will you forgive the enemy who has so grievously wounded you? Will you make sexual fidelity a matter of such importance that you'll order your life around it? Will you tell the truth even when it costs you money? Will you treat all people well, even those you don't need or don't like? These are a few of the things that Jesus did when he lived among us, and these are the things that he commands us to do. But most don't. When we face that moment of truth, the point in our story when Jesus calls us on to greater sacrifice, the moment when total allegiance is required, we press pause. We enjoy living in the fat middle age of the Christian life, secure in our identity as church members, involved parents, community boosters, Christians. Yet we know who signs the checks in our little economy, who sets the rules, who makes the choices — especially the hard ones between morality and satisfaction, honesty and security, integrity and humility — and it isn't God.

ɪɴᴛᴏ ᴛʜᴇ ʜᴀʀᴅ ᴘʟᴀᴄᴇꜱ

The word *authority* never sits well with people, especially Americans. Too many of our heroes are criminals, or at least law-defiers like Huckleberry Finn and Robin Hood. We're accustomed to thinking of the independent spirit as the model for living. We admire people who are tough, honest, fearless, and good but who are amenable not to family or culture or even the law but to their own code of right and wrong. That's us, we figure, doing what's right by our own reckoning, answerable to nothing but our own principles.

But that wasn't Jesus. Jesus lived as a person under authority. He did not his own will but the will of the Father. "I didn't come to be waited on," he said, "but to serve." His first temptation, and his final one, was to place his own desires ahead of the purpose that the Father had established for him. He refused to do so. "Not my will but yours be done," Jesus prayed. Then he surrendered his body and soul. To do the will of God is always to forfeit your own will. Just as Jesus lived under the authority of the Father, so we live under his authority. We do things his way, not our way. "If you obey my commands," Jesus said, "you will remain in my love, just as I have obeyed my Father's commands and remain in his love." A Christian is somebody who accepts the authority of Christ not part of the time or even most of the time but all of the time.

This means that sooner or later those of us who would take the name *Christian* will find ourselves up against a hard choice. We are almost certain to face a circumstance where what we think wise and best or what we just plain want the most is obviously different from the example and teaching of Jesus Christ. Authentic followers of Jesus Christ take his words seriously. They ponder commands like "Bless those who curse you" and do not reject them out of hand. They think about things like suffering and war and AIDS and poverty, and they ask in complete seriousness, "What would Jesus do about these things, and what would he have me do?" They believe that what one does with these very real, frightening, terrible things is not somehow separate from what it means to be a Christian. Rather it is precisely what it means to be a follower of Jesus. What is realistic? What is doable? These are the questions of Judas. A Christian realizes that one either follows Jesus or one does not. There is never a question of practicality, achievability, or even survivability. The only question is "What is the will of the Father in heaven?"

But that's hard to do.

Of course it is. Yet I doubt that Jesus, who placed himself so fully under the Father's authority that he submitted to crucifixion, will have patience with whiners and deadbeats who claim that they are fully submissive to God but constantly make excuses for having their own way. If we are not willing to apply Jesus' teaching to the hard things in life, then by Jesus' own pronouncement we are not Christians at all, let alone authentic ones. "I never knew you" is the greeting we can expect to receive the next time we meet.

This is a disturbing thought for low-pain-tolerance believers like me, who are attracted by whatever good things Jesus provides but are uninterested in submitting to his authority. Oddly, Jesus has always allowed these hangers-on to surround him and even to enter his inner circle. It is common to see followers of Jesus who merely use his name or as a basis for raising money or to lend credibility to their political cause but have no intention of accepting his authority in their lives. They have no intention of following Jesus as Peter did, into the Garden and even into the courtyard. If Peter denied Jesus in that hard place, it can mean only that he first went there with Jesus. Many never do.

I surrender ALL

Old Sister Mitchell died and had a glorious homegoing, as we used to call the funeral of a Christian. There was lots of shouting and hankie waving and singing songs of victory. She was ushered into heaven on the prayers of the saints. Well, as far as I know anyway. I'm believing that she gave

God greater authority in her life than she gave to the poor Pilgrim Holiness preacher with no television set. After the funeral, her portable TV—along with her other worldly goods—was sold off by a nephew. He had a garage sale to dispose of the white elephants that seemed so precious to her. How many of the things that we place even between ourselves and God are really items for the Goodwill?

And my family fared well enough without the black-and-white TV. We got a new television not long after that—a color TV. I think my dad now has about four of them. I myself own six, plus four computers. As a bonus, my father has been able to tell that story for years, using it to regale audiences as he makes a point about devoting oneself fully to God. For a preacher, there are no bad experiences, just great stories.

For what it's worth, I later gave up television for a period of about seven years. I had grown tired of its incessant noise, belligerent humor, and questionable influence on my children. I, too, sold my TV in a garage sale. Then, like Sister Mitchell, I began to miss my favorite shows. "It's just for football," I said when I brought home a brand-new color TV. The old lady was right about this much: television is a very hard thing to give away.

I aim to do better at surrendering my life to God.

aΓτerworD

"Go and do likewise."

J esus said, "Love your enemies."
So why don't we? Why do we not value humility and peacemaking more than we do? Why don't we
trust God more and love money less?

It may be, in part, because we believe these things to
be impossible. Our critique of Jesus' teaching is that it's
a nice bit of poetry but has little to do with real life. The
Beatitudes are lovely, but the world is a hard place,
dirty and real. Here there are such things as injustice

If we take seriously that during the Incarnation he was truly man, truly human as we are, then anything he did in his lifetime is available to us, too.

—MADELEINE L'ENGLE

and temptation and hard choices. Here there are real enemies. Perfection may be our ideal, but we do what we must to survive. Nobody's perfect, after all.

Yet Jesus was. He lived exactly as he taught us to live, absolutely unconcerned for self and utterly dependent upon the grace of God. He died, of course. But we all will die. Those who by pillaging the planet and exploiting others are able to extend their lives a little beyond Jesus' thirty-three years do not have grander lives, only longer ones. Jesus showed us a better way to live—and to die. And then he told us to do it. Did he ask us to do the impossible? Did he expect that we would fail?

To follow Jesus truly and not merely in name, we must believe that the things he calls us to do—the things he himself did—are not impossible or even improbable but normal for citizens of the Kingdom.

So I repent of my selfishness and cowardice, and I resolve to take Jesus at his word. I will believe that his words are trustworthy, his example is true, and there is no better thing I can do with my life than to live as he did. What he has called me to do, I will do. As he has forgiven my sins, I will forgive others. As he has washed my feet, I will serve others. As he has shown mercy to the poor, compassion on the sick, and anger toward the unjust, I will do likewise. I will laugh with my friends, cry with my enemies, honor my promises, hold money loosely, tell the truth at all times, renounce retribution, and tolerate all things but my own sin. I will love God with my whole heart. I will live a full life and die a good death, just as Jesus did.

Will you?

THE sermon on THE mounT

THE BEATITUDES

Now when he saw the crowds, he went up on a mountainside and sat down. His disciples came to him, and he began to teach them, saying:

> "Blessed are the poor in spirit,
>   for theirs is the kingdom of heaven.
> Blessed are those who mourn,

for they will be comforted.

Blessed are the meek,

    for they will inherit the earth.

Blessed are those who hunger and thirst for righteousness,

    for they will be filled.

Blessed are the merciful,

    for they will be shown mercy.

Blessed are the pure in heart,

    for they will see God.

Blessed are the peacemakers,

    for they will be called sons of God.

Blessed are those who are persecuted because of righteousness,

    for theirs is the kingdom of heaven.

"Blessed are you when people insult you, persecute you and falsely say all kinds of evil against you because of me. Rejoice and be glad, because great is your reward in heaven, for in the same way they persecuted the prophets who were before you.

SALT AND LIGHT

"You are the salt of the earth. But if the salt loses its saltiness, how can it be made salty again? It is no longer good for anything, except to be thrown out and trampled by men.

"You are the light of the world. A city on a hill cannot be hidden. Neither do people light a lamp and put it under a bowl. Instead they put it on its stand, and it gives light to everyone in the house. In the same way, let your light shine before men, that they may see your good deeds and praise your Father in heaven."

THE FULFILLMENT OF THE LAW

"Do not think that I have come to abolish the Law or the Prophets; I have not come to abolish them but to fulfill them. I tell you the truth, until heaven and earth disappear, not the smallest letter, not the least stroke of a pen, will by any means disappear from the Law until everything is accomplished. Anyone who breaks one of the least of these commandments and teaches others to do the same will be called least in the kingdom of heaven, but whoever practices and teaches these commands will be called great in the kingdom of heaven. For I tell you that unless your righteousness surpasses that of the Pharisees and the teachers of the law, you will certainly not enter the kingdom of heaven.

MURDER

"You have heard that it was said to the people long ago, 'Do not murder, and anyone who murders will be subject to judgment.' But I tell you that anyone who is angry with his brother will be subject to judgment. Again, anyone who says to his brother, 'Raca,' is answerable to the Sanhedrin. But anyone who says, 'You fool!' will be in danger of the fire of hell.

"Therefore, if you are offering your gift at the altar and there remember that your brother has something against you, leave your gift there in front of the altar. First go and be reconciled to your brother; then come and offer your gift.

"Settle matters quickly with your adversary who is taking you to court. Do it while you are still with him on the way, or he may hand you over to the judge, and the judge may hand you over to the officer, and you may be thrown into prison. I tell you the truth, you will not get out until you have paid the last penny.

ADULTErY

"You have heard that it was said, 'Do not commit adultery.' But I tell you that anyone who looks at a woman lustfully has already committed adultery with her in his heart. If your right eye causes you to sin, gouge it out and throw it away. It is better for you to lose one part of your body than for your whole body to be thrown into hell. And if your right hand causes you to sin, cut it off and throw it away. It is better for you to lose one part of your body than for your whole body to go into hell.

Divorce

"It has been said, 'Anyone who divorces his wife must give her a certificate of divorce.' But I tell you that anyone who divorces his wife, except for marital unfaithfulness, causes her to become an adulteress, and anyone who marries the divorced woman commits adultery.

Oaths

"Again, you have heard that it was said to the people long ago, 'Do not break your oath, but keep the oaths you have made to the Lord.' But I tell you, Do not swear at all: either by heaven, for it is God's throne; or by the earth, for it is his footstool; or by Jerusalem, for it is the city of the Great King. And do not swear by your head, for you cannot make even one hair white or black. Simply let your 'Yes' be 'Yes,' and your 'No,' 'No'; anything beyond this comes from the evil one.

An Eye for an Eye

"You have heard that it was said, 'Eye for eye, and tooth for tooth.' But I tell you, Do not resist an evil person. If someone strikes you on the right cheek, turn to him the other also. And if someone wants to sue you and take your tunic, let him have your cloak as well. If someone forces you to go one mile, go with him two miles. Give to the one who asks you, and do not turn away from the one who wants to borrow from you.

Love For Enemies

"You have heard that it was said, 'Love your neighbor and hate your enemy.' But I tell you: Love your enemies and pray for those who persecute you, that you may be sons of your Father in heaven. He causes his sun to rise on the evil and the good, and sends rain on the righteous and the unrighteous. If you love those who love you, what reward will you get? Are not even the tax collectors doing that? And if you greet only your brothers, what are you doing more than others? Do not even pagans do that? Be perfect, therefore, as your heavenly Father is perfect.

Giving To The Needy

"Be careful not to do your 'acts of righteousness' before men, to be seen by them. If you do, you will have no reward from your Father in heaven.

"So when you give to the needy, do not announce it with trumpets, as the hypocrites do in the synagogues and on the streets, to be honored by men. I tell you the truth, they have received their reward in full. But when you give to the needy, do not let your left hand know what your right hand is doing, so that your giving may be in secret. Then your Father, who sees what is done in secret, will reward you.

prayer

"And when you pray, do not be like the hypocrites, for they love to pray standing in the synagogues and on the street corners to be seen by men. I tell you the truth, they have received their reward in full. But when you pray, go into your room, close the door and pray to your Father, who is unseen. Then your Father, who sees what is done in secret, will reward you. And when you pray, do not keep on babbling like pagans, for they think they will be heard because of their many words. Do not be like them, for your Father knows what you need before you ask him.

"This, then, is how you should pray:

> "'Our Father in heaven,
> hallowed be your name,
> your kingdom come,
> your will be done on earth as it is in heaven.
> Give us today our daily bread.
> Forgive us our debts, as we also have forgiven our debtors.
> And lead us not into temptation,
> but deliver us from the evil one.'

For if you forgive men when they sin against you, your heavenly Father will also forgive you. But if you do not forgive men their sins, your Father will not forgive your sins.

FaSTINg

"When you fast, do not look somber as the hypocrites do, for they disfigure their faces to show men they are fasting. I tell you the truth, they have received their reward in full. But when you fast, put oil on your head and wash your face, so that it will not be obvious to men that you are fasting, but only to your Father, who is unseen; and your Father, who sees what is done in secret, will reward you.

Treasures in Heaven

"Do not store up for yourselves treasures on earth, where moth and rust destroy, and where thieves break in and steal. But store up for yourselves treasures in heaven, where moth and rust do not destroy, and where thieves do not break in and steal. For where your treasure is, there your heart will be also.

"The eye is the lamp of the body. If your eyes are good, your whole body will be full of light. But if your eyes are bad, your whole body will be full of darkness. If then the light within you is darkness, how great is that darkness!

"No one can serve two masters. Either he will hate the one and love the other, or he will be devoted to the one and despise the other. You cannot serve both God and Money.

DO NOT WORRY

"Therefore I tell you, do not worry about your life, what you will eat or drink; or about your body, what you will wear. Is not life more important than food, and the body more important than clothes? Look at the birds of the air; they do not sow or reap or store away in barns, and yet your heavenly Father feeds them. Are you not much more valuable than they? Who of you by worrying can add a single hour to his life?

"And why do you worry about clothes? See how the lilies of the field grow. They do not labor or spin. Yet I tell you that not even Solomon in all his splendor was dressed like one of these. If that is how God clothes the grass of the field, which is here today and tomorrow is thrown into the fire, will he not much more clothe you, O you of little faith? So do not worry, saying, 'What shall we eat?' or 'What shall we drink?' or 'What shall we wear?' For the pagans run after all these things, and your heavenly Father knows that you need them. But seek first his kingdom and his righteousness, and all these things will be given to you as well. Therefore do not worry about tomorrow, for tomorrow will worry about itself. Each day has enough trouble of its own.

JUDGING OTHERS

"Do not judge, or you too will be judged. For in the same way you judge others, you will be judged, and with the measure you use, it will be measured to you.

"Why do you look at the speck of sawdust in your brother's eye and pay no attention to the plank in your own eye? How can you say to your brother, 'Let me take the speck out of your eye,' when all the time there is a plank in your own eye? You hypocrite, first take the plank out of your own eye, and then you will see clearly to remove the speck from your brother's eye.

"Do not give dogs what is sacred; do not throw your pearls to pigs. If you do, they may trample them under their feet, and then turn and tear you to pieces.

ASK, SEEK, KNOCK

"Ask and it will be given to you; seek and you will find; knock and the door will be opened to you. For everyone who asks receives; he who seeks finds; and to him who knocks, the door will be opened.

"Which of you, if his son asks for bread, will give him a stone? Or if he asks for a fish, will give him a snake? If you, then, though you are evil, know how to give good gifts to your children, how much more will your Father in heaven give good gifts to those who ask him! So in everything, do to others what you would have them do to you, for this sums up the Law and the Prophets.

THE Narrow and wide Gates

"Enter through the narrow gate. For wide is the gate and broad is the road that leads to destruction, and many enter through it. But small is the gate and narrow the road that leads to life, and only a few find it.

A Tree and its Fruit

"Watch out for false prophets. They come to you in sheep's clothing, but inwardly they are ferocious wolves. By their fruit you will recognize them. Do people pick grapes from thornbushes, or figs from thistles? Likewise every good tree bears good fruit, but a bad tree bears bad fruit. A good tree cannot bear bad fruit, and a bad tree cannot bear good fruit. Every tree that does not bear good fruit is cut down and thrown into the fire. Thus, by their fruit you will recognize them.

"Not everyone who says to me, 'Lord, Lord,' will enter the kingdom of heaven, but only he who does the will of my Father who is in heaven. Many will say to me on that day, 'Lord, Lord, did we not prophesy in your name, and in your name drive out demons and perform many miracles?' Then I will tell them plainly, 'I never knew you. Away from me, you evildoers!'

THE WISE AND FOOLISH BUILDERS

"Therefore everyone who hears these words of mine and puts them into practice is like a wise man who built his house on the rock. The rain came down, the streams rose, and the winds blew and beat against that house; yet it did not fall, because it had its foundation on the rock. But everyone who hears these words of mine and does not put them into practice is like a foolish man who built his house on sand. The rain came down, the streams rose, and the winds blew and beat against that house, and it fell with a great crash."

When Jesus had finished saying these things, the crowds were amazed at his teaching, because he taught as one who had authority, and not as their teachers of the law.

DISCUSSION GUIDE

HOW TO LEAD A GROUP IN LEARNING
FROM THIS BOOK

One of the best ways to learn from reading is to share the experience with a group of friends. Hearing their reactions and insights—and sharing your own—will help you critique the author's point of view and sharpen your own thinking. You'll come away with firmer convictions about, in this case, what it means to be a follower of Jesus Christ.

Your group can be small. Three or four people is enough to start; groups of fewer than a dozen usually work best. Meet at your home, a coffee shop, library, or any informal setting. Begin by setting a time and location for your first gathering and asking a few acquaintances to join you.

You don't need a leader. Someone may emerge as a moderator to guide the discussion, or you could rotate that responsibility among the members. At your first meeting, settle on the logistics of the group—where and when you'll meet, whether you'll bring snacks, and other practical matters. It's usually best to agree at the outset how many times the group will gather.

The following discussion guide reviews the major ideas of this book under four topics. This could be used as a four-session template, or the group could decide to meet for a shorter or longer period of time by either selecting just a few relevant questions or discussing each topic in more detail. Remember that the strength of groups like this is participation. Create an atmosphere in which everyone feels welcome to share his or her opinion, and try to avoid having one or two people dominate the discussion.

Also remember that there will be an unseen visitor at your gatherings—God. As you meet, open your mind to him and the truth he may reveal either through this book or through the comments of your group members.

At some time during each of your gatherings, allow time to consider this important question: *How would my life change if I understood the teaching of Jesus Christ more clearly and took them more seriously?* Ultimately, your group's purpose is not to learn about this book or its author—it is to know Jesus and to become more like him.

TOPIC one: WHAT IS a CHrISTIan?

1. What does the word *Christian* mean to you?

2. Which of the following sources contribute most to your understanding of the term?

   - The teachings of the church
   - World history
   - Your own experience
   - The Bible
   - Reason
   - The words or example of people who are Christians
   - Something else

3. Do you consider yourself a Christian? If so, which of the following best describes your understanding of what Christianity is?

   - An experience
   - A decision

- A lifestyle
- A heritage
- A culture
- A ritual
- Something else

4. The author strongly asserts that Jesus Christ himself provides the only valid definition of the term *Christian*. Do you agree or disagree? What is your reasoning?

5. If Christianity were defined primarily by examining the life and teachings of Jesus Christ, how closely would that definition match the most common expressions of Christianity seen in your community? In what ways would it be the same? How might it be different?

6. List some of the commonly used modifiers for the term *Christian* or *Christianity,* such as *evangelical, fundamentalist, emergent,* and *mainline.* Can you name others? In your opinion, what do these terms add to an understanding of Christianity? Do you find them helpful? Neutral? Distracting?

7. What habits or practices tend to strengthen one's association with Jesus Christ? What habits or practices tend to weaken it?

8. How does being a Christian affect the way you think? How does it affect your behavior?

9. After reading this book, are you more or less likely to identify yourself as a Christian?

10. How would your life change if you understood the teaching of Jesus Christ more clearly and took them more seriously?

TOPIC TWO:
WHAT MAKES CHRISTIANS DIFFERENT FROM OTHERS?

1. Summarize your philosophy of life in a single sentence. In other words, what is the bumper-sticker version of your worldview? Here are some examples—

   • Life is short; play hard.
   • Got chocolate?
   • Visualize world peace.

2. Describe the dominant culture that exists in each of the following settings. In other words, what operating principles or values do you most often see applied in these places?

- Your school

- Your workplace

- Your home

- Your family of origin

- Your church

3. Read the Beatitudes, found in Matthew 5:1–11, or, if you have a bit more time, read the entire Sermon on the Mount (see page 199). Summarize the worldview that you see illustrated there. In what ways is it similar to the worldview you encounter at school, work, or among others? In what ways is it different?

4. In what ways is the worldview seen in the Beatitudes similar to your own way of thinking? In what ways is it different?

5. The author asserts that Jesus' philosophy of life contrasts so sharply with the way most people think that it would be considered crazy by an average person. Do you agree? Why or why not?

6. Is Jesus' way of thinking practical? In other words, could a person reasonably be expected to live by this philosophy? Explain your reasoning.

7. Jesus labeled his way of thinking about life as a kingdom, the *kingdom of heaven*. Can you think of another metaphor to describe what it means to follow Jesus?

8. If we accept the idea that followers of Christ are members of an alternative kingdom or culture, what are the implications for their involvement in the broader culture in which they live? In other words, how should Christians view themselves in relation to their community? Their nation?

9. The author describes a moment when he determined to put "both feet in," declaring a complete allegiance to Jesus. Have you ever made a similar declaration? Do you think it is necessary to finally choose one or the other, as this author states?

10. If you are were to make such a declaration of allegiance of Jesus Christ, what, if anything, would have to change about the way you think or live?

TOPIC THREE: WHAT DOES IT MEAN TO LOVE OTHERS?

1. Why is it so hard for people to accept one another and get along? What might solve this problem?

2. Glance through the Sermon on the Mount (see pages 199–210). List some of the teachings that have to do with interpersonal relationships. Summarize the advice that Jesus gave.

3. Do you think it is realistic for a person to actually forgive someone who has committed a great wrong or to love an enemy? Why or why not?

4. Do you see a difference between tolerance for a person and approval of that person's behavior? Between forgiveness and exoneration? Between nonviolence and permission? If so, define the difference(s).

5. What do you think it means to forgive? What does it mean to love an enemy?

6. Of the personal relationships you are involved in, which one presents the greatest challenge to you? Would you consider this person or people to be an enemy?

7. Based on Jesus' teaching, what is your responsibility in amending this relationship? What is the other person's responsibility?

8. Do you think Jesus' teachings on tolerance, forgiveness, and nonviolence should be applied to groups of people as well as to individuals? Explain your thinking.

9. How would the relationships in your life change if you were better able to apply Jesus teachings to your life?

10. Is there anyone that you should forgive? Is there anyone from whom you have the need to seek forgiveness? Are you willing to do that? When and how will you do so?

TOPIC FOUr:
IS IT POSSIBLe TO LIVe as Jesus DID?

1. Do you think that Jesus' teachings are to be taken literally, figuratively, or in some other way? Why do you think so?

2. Many people believe that Jesus' more rigorous teachings are impractical and would be impossible to enact in the real world. Do you agree? Why or why not?

3. How consistently did Jesus apply his own teachings to life? What was the result?

4. What advice would you give for a person who had heard Jesus' teachings for the first time and was eager to implement them?

5. Do you believe that God is personal? In other words, do you believe that it is possible for individual people to interact with God one-to-one through prayer or some other means?

6. What support systems—such as friends, family, church, or prayer—assist you in your attempt to become a follower of Jesus Christ? Explain the benefit that they provide.

7. Which would be better, a world in which good people acted with kindness and humility but were subjugated by evil people, or a world in which good people used brutality and deception to keep evil people in check? Explain your thinking.

8. What kind of world do you envision in the future? Will it be better or worse? More violent or more peaceful? What part, if any, will your behavior and lifestyle play in making that vision real?

9. How would your life change if you understood the life and teachings of Jesus better and applied them more fully?

10. What would be the next step for you to take in becoming a fully devoted follower of Jesus Christ? Are you willing to take it? When?

note
ᴛᴏ readers

DON'T LET THIS BOOK
SIT On a SHELF!

No book is meant to gather dust, and this one especially is designed to be put to work. It's purpose is to provoke thought, generate discussion, and help people discover what it means to be a Christian.

You can help it accomplish that.

If you liked this book and found it helpful in your spiritual journey, pass it on to a friend. If you didn't like the book or disagreed with what it says, consider giving it to a friend anyway—at the very least, it will give you a starting point for discussing what it means to be a Christian. Even a bad book can be useful.

Either way, I'd like to hear your reaction. You can get in touch with me at www.lawrencewilson.com.

—LAWRENCE W. WILSON
JOHN 20:31